GUIDE TO THE FEDERAL COURTS

An Introduction to the Federal Courts and Their Operation

Includes Explanation of How a Case is Litigated

WANT Publishing Company
1511 K Street, N.W.
Washington, DC 20005

All rights reserved.
Printed by Catterton Printing Co.,
  Washington, D.C., United States of America
ISBN 0-942008-02-2

Library of Congress Catalog Card Number: 81-70747

330646

GUIDE TO THE FEDERAL COURTS

TABLE OF CONTENTS

TABLE OF CONTENTS (Continued)

page

INTRODUCTION

The United States has a dual court structure — a federal judiciary system, and a court system operated by each of the states. While most litigation occurs at the state court level, the federal courts are playing an ever larger role in the resolution of disputes. This is due in part to Congress, which in recent years has enacted a wide range of new laws that grant citizen access to the federal courts. It is due also in part to an increase in cases filed in more long-standing areas of federal litigation.

During the past decade, the number of cases filed in federal courts around the country has more than doubled. Hardly a day goes by when a federal court action — be it that of the U.S. Supreme Court or a lower federal court — does not make front page news.

GUIDE TO THE FEDERAL COURTS is intended as an introduction to the federal judiciary and as a guide to how the federal courts operate. It will examine, in easy-to-read format, the kinds of cases being heard by the federal, as opposed to the state, courts and the operation of our three-tiered federal system, which includes the Supreme Court, the Court of Appeals, and the District Courts. It will also look at the special courts in the federal system, including the Court of Claims, the Court of International Trade, the Tax Court, and others.

GUIDE TO THE FEDERAL COURTS will, in addition, examine, on a step-by-step basis, how a case is litigated in federal court, tracking a federal case from the time it is filed until it is disposed of, by decision or settlement. Two examples, one involving a products liability case and another an antitrust (unfair trade) case will be used for this purpose.

GUIDE TO THE FEDERAL COURTS will also look at a number of current issues relating to the federal courts, including, among others, class action lawsuits, latent disease (toxic substance) actions, and the problems of court delay. A special Glossary of Terms is given in Appendix I. (See detailed Table of Contents above.)

The objective here is to give the reader an appreciation and basic understanding of the federal judicial system. The federal system has grown to the point that no citizen can afford to be without some knowledge as to how it operates. The step-by-step examination of how a case is litigated in federal court can also be applied to most state judicial systems.

PART I

THE FEDERAL COURT SYSTEM

Cases Subject to Federal Jurisdiction

There are two sets of judicial systems in the United States. One set is that of the state and local courts established in each of the 50 states under the authority of that particular state's constitution and statutory law. The other is that of the United States courts, established by the Congress of the United States, pursuant to authority vested in it by the Constitution.[1]

The state courts have general, unlimited power to decide almost every type of civil and criminal case, subject to limitations imposed by state law and to preemption by federal law.

The state courts, in fact, handle the bulk of the nation's legal matters. State judiciary systems are the primary forums for such proceedings as criminal prosecutions, divorce actions and the probate of estates, as well as most cases involving commercial transactions (e.g., the enforcement of business contracts) and personal injury/product liability. The federal courts, however, have seen their jurisdiction expand considerably over the years —- particularly so during the past decade — and now have a much more significant role to play in the overall litigation picture.

This existence of a dual court structure, Federal-State, is a distinguishing feature of our American judicial system.

Under the U.S. Constitution, the federal government is set forth as a government of enumerated powers. The states retain power in those fields not pre-empted by the federal government. The question as to when the federal government can exercise authority over the states, and when the federal courts can assume jurisdiction over otherwise state and local matters is a recurrent problem, and perhaps an inherent one in our dual system. The U.S. Supreme Court, for example, has long grappled with the question of whether and to what extent a federal court hearing should be available to a plaintiff alleging constitutional violations, such as illegal search and seizure, when the claim has already been decided against him by a state court.

While some constitutional and other issues facing the courts will be discussed, our main objective here is to describe — in easy-to-read format — the basic framework in which the federal courts operate and how a federal court case is heard and tried. Much of this discussion will apply, by analogy, to the state court litigation process.

Diversity Jurisdiction

Most of the nation's litigation, as indicated, occurs at the state level. When a person has a grievance, he generally can be assured that there is a state court,

---

[1]The basic authority for the fedeal judicial system is contained in Article III of the Constitution which provides that "The judicial power of the United States shall be vested in one Supreme Court, and in such inferior courts as the Congress may from time to time ordain and establish..."

be it a small claims court or a court of general sessions, that will consider his case.

While federal courts are playing a larger role in the total litigation picture, federal courts are limited — by Congressional enactment — as to the cases over which they can accept jurisdiction. In order for a case to be filed in federal court —that is, for a federal court to accept jurisdiction over the matter — at least one of two general conditions must prevail. Either there must be diversity of citizenship, or a federal question must be involved. These two conditions for federal jurisdiction will be taken up in turn.

Diversity jurisdiction refers to suits between citizens from different states. The rationale behind diversity jurisdiction is that it may be difficult for a non-resident defendant to receive a fair trial if the plaintiff brought suit in his own state court. The amount in controversy for diversity to apply must be at least $10,000. That is, even though the case may involve citizens of different states, the plaintiff must claim at least $10,000 in damages in order for a federal court to accept jurisdiction.

Suppose, for example, a citizen of South Carolina was involved in an automobile accident in his home state in which the other party was from North Carolina. Suppose, also, that the South Carolina driver claims the North Carolina driver was negligent. Since there is no federal law involving driver negligence, this kind of lawsuit would normally be a matter for the state courts to decide. But because the parties happen to be from different states and diversity jurisdiction would apply (assuming the amount in controversy was at least $10,000), a federal forum would also be available. The South Carolina plaintiff could bring the suit in either federal or state court. If he brought it in a South Carolina state court (as he is likely to do), the defendant, on the basis of diversity, could remove the action to the fedral court that has jurisdiction over that particular area. (See Figure 1, p. 4.) The federal court, in resolving the case, would apply state law.

Another and very common example of cases in federal court on the basis of diversity jurisdiction are products liability actions. Suppose a citizen of Iowa is injured by a product manufactured in Illinois. Since there is no federal law governing products liability, this would normally be a matter for the state courts (it could probably be filed in either of the two states). But since diversity applies, a federal forum would also be available; if the (allegedly) injured plaintiff filed in state court, the defendant would have the right of removal to federal court.

In addition to considerations of local prejudice, other reasons an attorney may decide to remove a case to federal court (if the plaintiff files in state court) include generally crowded state calendars and certain advantages that may pertain to federal, as opposed to state, court procedures.

A few more words on diversity jurisdiction. The diversity required is complete diversity. For example, if two citizens, one from New York and one from New Jersey, join in a suit against a citizen of New Jersey, there is no diversity, since one of the plaintiffs is a citizen of the same state as the defendant. The case would, therefore, have to be heard in state court. On the other hand, where the party joined in a suit is not necessary to its being litigated (i.e., the suit can proceed without him) and his presence defeats complete diversity, he may be dropped by the court in order to effect complete diversity, and thus allow for

Figure 1

UNITED STATES COURTS OF APPEALS and UNITED STATES DISTRICT COURTS

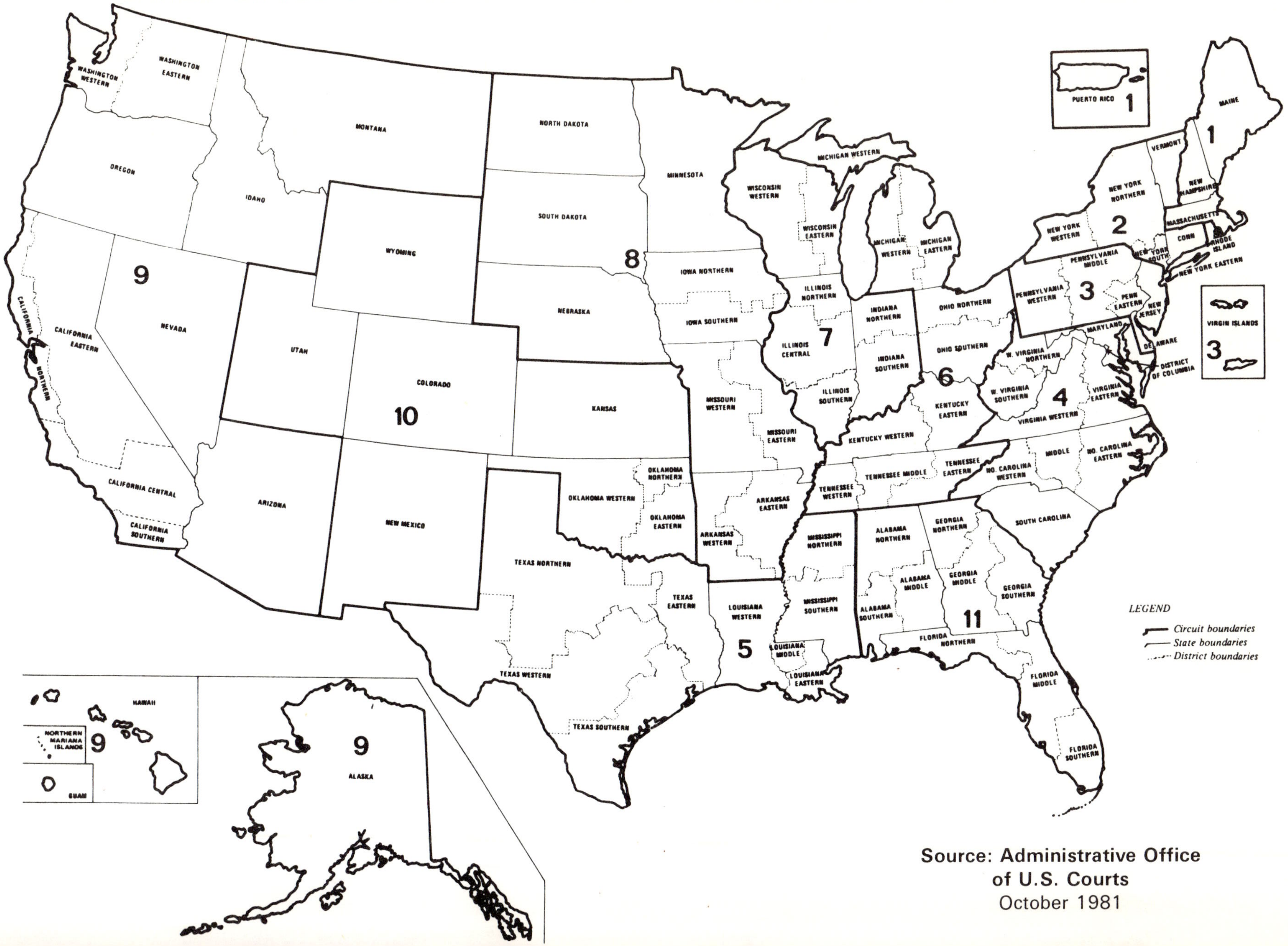

Source: Administrative Office
of U.S. Courts
October 1981

LEGEND
Circuit boundaries
State boundaries
District boundaries

federal court jurisdiction. For diversity purposes, a corporation is considered to be a citizen of the state in which it is incorporated *and* of the state where it has its principal place of business.

A recent U.S. Supreme Court decision, however, has made it somewhat easier for a certain type of multiparty action to achieve diversity status even though complete diversity may not actually prevail.[1] The Court held that trustees of an investment trust may sue in federal district court regardless of the state citizenship of the trust's beneficiaries. Prior to this decision, lower federal courts had been taking into account each shareholder's citizenship, the range of which usually prevented the complete diversity between opposing parties required for federal jurisdiction. As a result, litigants in such cases were often limited to state courts.

Approximately 25% of all civil cases filed in federal district courts around the country involve diversity jurisdiction. That is, one-fourth of all actions, either brought in federal court or removed to federal court by the defendant, would otherwise have been heard at the state level but for the fact that the parties happened to be from different states.

Federal Question Jurisdiction

The other basis for litigating a case in federal court is referred to as "federal question" jurisdiction. That is, an action alleging a violation of federal statutory law, as set forth in the U.S. Code, may properly be filed in federal court. For some alleged violations of the Code, federal courts are to have exclusive jurisdiction (i.e., the litigants are limited to a federal forum); for others, the litigants may sue in either federal or state court. Several federal environmental statutes, for example, allow certain actions to be filed in either a federal or state forum.

The number of cases filed in federal court on the basis of federal question jurisdiction has shown rapid increase in recent years. In 1980, over 75,000 such federal question cases were filed in U.S. district courts across the country, more than twice the number filed in 1970. This increase is due in part to a gain in new cases filed in traditional areas of federal litigation, such as antitrust/unfair trade, labor, and securities, and in part to recent legislation creating new federal causes of action in areas where none before existed. During the past decade, in fact, over 70 such new laws have been enacted, including statutes relating to the environment, equal employment, housing, and pension reform. Under the federal clean air and water acts, for example, a citizen may bring a suit in U.S. district court if he feels environmental requirements are not being met. The Equal Employment Opportunity Act allows an individual to bring a federal court action when he feels he has been the victim of job discrimination on the basis of race, sex, national origin, or religion. The Employee Retirement Income Security Act allows an individual to challenge in federal court certain practices in regard to the pension program set up by his employer.

Federal question cases will be further examined below. A survey of selected, recently-filed federal question cases is given in Appendix II.

Three-Tiered Court System

The U.S. Constitution provides far more detail on the make-up of the Executive

---

[1] Navarro Savings Assoc. v. Lee, #79-465, May 9, 1980.

and Legislative branches of the Federal Government than the Judicial. Concerning the last, the only court mandated by the Constitution is the Supreme Court. The Congress, however, based on discretionary authority granted in the Constitution, has from time to time established the various other United States courts, such as the U.S. appellate and district courts and the various federal special courts.

The United States court system may be likened to a pyramid. At the apex of the pyramid stands the Supreme Court of the United States, the highest court in the land. On the next level stand the U.S. courts of appeals, 12 in all. On the next level stand the U.S. district courts, 94 in all, including the U.S. district courts for the District of Columbia and Puerto Rico and the district courts in the Canal Zone, Guam, and the Virgin Islands. (See Fig. 1, p. 4.) Also, there are special federal courts, established for a specific purpose, including the Court of Claims, the Tax Court, and others. (See below section entitled "Special Courts," p. 14.)

Within the federal judiciary system, lawsuits generally begin in the U.S. district courts, which are the trial courts of the federal system, or in one of the special courts, such as the Court of Claims. The major exception to this involves appeals from agency determinations, which, in many instances, by-pass the district courts and go directly to the appropriate U.S. court of appeals. An appeal from a decision of the Federal Trade Commission, for example, would go directly to the Court of Appeals level. The same applies to rulings by the National Labor Relations Board and most other executive departments and independent agencies.

Thus, for the most part, a party involved in a federal lawsuit may proceed through three levels of decision. His case will be initially tried and decided by a federal district court (or federal agency). If either party is dissatisfied with the decision rendered, he may appeal to one of the 12 U.S. courts of appeals. The next, and final, level of appeal is the U.S. Supreme Court. A party may petition the Supreme Court to review an appeals court decision — this is known as a "petition for certiorari" — but the Court is not obligated to hear and decide such cases.[1] In fact, only a small percentage of petitions for certiorari are granted.

This pyramidal organization of the federal court system is mirrored by many state judicial systems. A few states have a two-tiered rather than a three-tiered system.

The U.S. Supreme Court

The highest court in the federal system is the Supreme Court of the United States. It consists of nine justices, appointed for life by the President with the advice and consent of the U.S. Senate. One justice is designated Chief Justice. The current Chief Justice is Warren E. Burger, who has held the position since 1969.

The complete membership of the Court, as of March 1982, is as follows: (The

---

[1]By act of Congress, the Supreme Court is required to hear only certain types of appeals from the federal appeals courts and state supreme courts. Basically, such cases must involve a federal statute being held unconstitutional or a state statute being held unconstitutional or repugnant to state law.

President that appointed each Justice is given in parentheses.)

Warren E. Burger, Chief	(Nixon)
William J. Brennan, Jr.	(Eisenhower)
Byron R. White	(Kennedy)
Thurgood Marshall	(Johnson)
Harry A. Blackmun	(Nixon)
Lewis F. Powell, Jr.	(Nixon)
William H. Rehnquist	(Nixon)
John Paul Stevens	(Ford)
Sandra Day O'Connor	(Reagan)

The Court meets on the first Monday of October each year. It continues in session usually until June and generally disposes of upwards of 5000 cases each year. In most of these cases the Court refuses to accept certiorari. That is, the Court says it will not further review the lower court opinion in the matter. In approximately 150 cases each year, the Court accepts review, hears arguments on the issues involved, and hands down written opinions.

As indicated, in the great majority of cases filed before it, the Supreme Court denies certiorari and the lower court opinion stands and controls the law in the area of that particular court's jurisdiction. If, for instance, that lower court was the U.S. Circuit Court of Appeals for the Seventh Circuit, then that court's decision in the case is determinative in the states of Illinois, Indiana, and Wisconsin — the states that make up the Seventh Circuit. (See Fig. 1, p. 4.) Other circuits, however, may have decided differently on the same issue, and a different rule of law may prevail.

Since the Supreme Court accepts only a small percentage of the cases filed before it for full review and decision, it tries to accept those that raise issues of great national importance and in which there is a conflict among the circuits, i.e., different circuit courts have decided differently on the same issue. Four Supreme Court Justices must vote to accept certiorari before the full Court can hear and decide the case. If fewer than four justices vote to hear a case, then certiorari is denied and the lower court opinion stands.

Legislation is pending in Congress that would establish a National Court of Appeals to hear certain cases in which the Supreme Court denies certiorari. Under one proposal, the National Court of Appeals would consist of nine justices and hear only those cases referred to it by the Supreme Court. Proponents of the new court argue that it is desperately needed to relieve caseload burdens of the nation's highest court.

The Supreme Court in recent years has had to deal with a number of controversial issues, in which public opinion is sharply divided, such as on the issues of abortion, busing, and school prayer. A number of bills have been introduced in Congress that would prevent the Supreme Court from ruling on such questions, that is, remove such questions from Supreme Court and lower federal court jurisdiction. These bills are generally designed to counteract court decisions of the past decade, for example, those legalizing abortion and banning state-sponsored prayer. Such proposed legislation would allow only state courts to rule on these matters as each saw fit, thus ending the nationwide uniformity maintained by the Supreme Court.

While opinion is mixed, most constitutional scholars say that there is no law or Supreme Court ruling that would stop Congress from removing judicial authority in controversial areas. Congress' authority to remove federal jurisdiction, they point out, derives from Article III of the Constitution, which specifically provides that: "The Supreme Court shall have appellate jurisdiction, both as to law and fact, with such exceptions, and under such regulations as the Congress shall make." Though the question has never been fully tested, many agree that Congress, if it so desires, can do almost anything it wants in regard to the jurisdiction of the Supreme Court and the lower federal courts.

It appears unlikely that legislation along these lines will pass any time soon. While many concede the authority of Congress in this regard, they doubt the wisdom of stripping the federal courts of jurisdiction in a piece-meal fashion. A preferred way for achieving the same objective, they argue, would be a constitutional amendment. This procedure, however, requires a two-thirds vote of the House and Senate plus ratification by three-fourths of the states. Legislation to limit Supreme Court authority, on the other hand, would require for approval only a majority vote of Congress, and, of course, the President's signature.

In a different context, the authority of the Executive Branch to remove cases from federal court jurisdiction in certain emergency circumstances was recently upheld by the Supreme Court. The case involved actions taken by the President in striking a deal to end the Iranian hostage crisis, including an agreement on the part of the U.S. Government to terminate all legal proceedings in United States courts involving claims of U.S. citizens against Iran. The Supreme Court held that though there is no specific authorization for this action, such can be inferred from legislation on the books granting a President broad authority in dealing with an international crisis.[1]

Courts of Appeals

The intermediate appellate courts in the United States judicial system are the courts of appeals in 11 circuits plus the District of Columbia. Each circuit court of appeals includes three or more states, except the District of Columbia Circuit. The federal circuit and district court breakdowns are given in Figure 1 on page 4. The Fifth Circuit, as noted in Figure 1, has recently been split into two circuits: the (new) Fifth, consisting of Louisiana, Mississippi, and Texas; and the Eleventh, consisting of Alabama, Florida, Georgia, and the Canal Zone.

The appellate courts — also referred to as circuit courts or U.S. circuit courts of appeals — receive cases appealed from the U.S. district courts and from certain federal administrative agencies. Any appeals from circuit court opinions go, of course, to the U.S. Supreme Court.

During fiscal 1980 (the twelve month period ending September 30, 1980), 23,200 appeals were filed in the U.S. Courts of Appeals. This was an increase of 14.7 percent over 1979 and the largest increase over a previous year since 1962. The largest increase in fiscal 1980 were in appeals from federal district court extortion and racketeering cases on the criminal side and federal prisoner civil rights appeals on the civil side.

---

[1]*Dames & Moore v. Regan, Sec. of Treasury,* No. 80-2078, July 2, 1981.

Appeals from decisions of federal administrative agencies constitute about 13 percent of total cases filed in the circuit courts. Reviews by the circuits of NLRB decisions generated the most appeals from administrative agencies in fiscal 1980. Other agencies with a large number of appeals were the Internal Revenue Service, the Environmental Protection Agency, the Federal Energy Regulatory Commission, and Occupational Safety and Health Administration.

District Courts

Within the federal system, the U.S. district courts are where cases are initially filed and tried. There are 94 federal district courts, 89 in the 50 states, and one each in the District of Columbia, the Canal Zone, Guam, Puerto Rico, and the Virgin Islands. (See Fig. 1, p. 4.)

Each state has at least one federal court; but many states are divided into two or three districts, and California, Texas, and New York consist of four districts each. For each district, there is a clerk's office, a United States Marshal's office, and one or more bankruptcy judges, United States magistrates, probation officers and court reporters. In addition, each district has a United States Attorney's office.

A district court itself may be divided into divisions, each division representing a place where a case may be filed and/or tried. For example, the U.S. District Court for the Southern District of Florida, in addition to its main office in Miami, has divisional offices in Fort Lauderdale and West Palm Beach.

Federal Litigation

A suit filed in federal court may be civil or criminal in nature. While civil suits have shown a dramatic rise in the last decade, criminal actions (the Government, of course, is always the initiator, or plaintiff, in a criminal suit) have continued to decline, now representing only about 17 percent of the civil/criminal total. This does not, unfortunately, indicate a decrease in criminal activity. Quite the contrary has been the case. The decline in federal criminal prosecutions stems from the fact that the Government has been turning more prosecutions over to the states, particularly cases involving bank robberies and juvenile offenders. The Justice Department has recently announced a policy of focusing its criminal efforts in certain priority areas, such as organized crime, narcotics, public corruption and white-collar crime.

Overall, the bulk of criminal cases fall within the jurisdiction of state and local governments. It is estimated that only about six percent of criminal activity falls within the purview of federal statutes.

Let us look more closely at the civil side of federal court litigation. Civil cases refer to those actions in which the plaintiff seeks an injunction or money damages compensating for personal or economic loss. In a criminal case, on the other hand, the prosecutor (the ''plaintiff'' in a criminal case) seeks incarceration and/or fines. Most civil actions in federal district court involve private parties both as plaintiff and defendant, though the Government may also sue or be sued in a civil action. It should be noted that the same factual allegations may spur both civil and criminal lawsuits. If the Government, for instance, feels it has uncovered a serious antitrust conspiracy, it may bring a civil action seeking an injunction to halt such violations and concurrently bring a criminal action (based on a criminal information or a grand jury indictment[1]) asking stiff jail sentences for those involved. In addition, it is not unusual in such circumstances for private plaintiffs to file civil suits seeking damages against the defendants named in criminal Government actions.

There has been a dramatic rise in civil litigation in U.S. district courts during the past decade, such cases having doubled during that period. This increase, as indicated, is attributable both to lawsuits resulting from new federal statutes being enacted and to a rise in litigation in traditional areas, such as that based on diversity jurisdiction. In fiscal 1980, a total of 168,789 civil cases were filed in federal district courts around the country, an increase of 9.1 percent over 1979.

A breakdown of district court civil filings covering the six-year period 1975-1980 is given in Figure 2 on page 11. As indicated, breach of contract and tort actions numbered over 49,000 in fiscal 1980, an increase of 32.9 percent over 1979. About half of the cases filed in the Tort Actions category entitled "Other Personal Injury" represents products liability cases. Such cases in fiscal year 1980 numbered 7,755, an increase of 26.5 percent over the previous 12-month period.

As shown in Figure 2, Actions under (Federal) Statutes stood at 75,574 in fiscal 1980. This represents 45 percent of all civil cases filed in U.S. district courts in 1980. The number of cases filed under selected federal statutes include: Antitrust (1,496); Civil Rights (12,944); Labor Laws (8,640); Patent/Copyright/Trademark (3,783); Securities and Commodities (1,694); and Freedom of Information (627).

A full 31 percent of Actions under Statutes consists of prisoner petitions. Prisoner petitions involve either habeas corpus actions, i.e., claims by the prisoner that he is being wrongfully held, or civil rights actions. Most prisoner petitions, in fact, consist of civil rights claims alleging such violations as unsanitary prison conditions or cruel treatment by prison officials. In a recent case, a Maryland federal jury awarded over $1 million in damages to hundreds of people held in a county jail.[2] The verdict, unprecedented in its size and scope, was based on the jury's findings that the jail was chronically overcrowded and sometimes filthy.

Civil rights actions against the federal government by both prisoners and non-prisoners are based on the Civil Rights Act of 1871. The Act was passed after the Civil War to protect blacks from discrimination in the South and from terror as practiced by such groups as the Ku Klux Klan. But in recent years, due in part to decisions of the U.S. Supreme Court, the Act has been used in claims involving everything from police brutality to welfare check denials.

The "Other" listing under the Actions under Statutes category represents cases filed under such laws as those dealing with the environment, energy, and truth-in-lending.

---

[1]For explanation of legal terminology, see Appendix I — "Glossary of Terms." Also for general discussion of terms used in a criminal case, see section in Part II below entitled "Criminal Procedure."

[2]*Walker v. Galeone*, U.S. District Court for Maryland, HM-80-1889 (Oct. 1, 1981).

Figure 2

Civil Cases Commenced in the U.S. District Courts, by Nature of Suit, During the Twelve Month Period Ended June 30, 1975 - 1980

Nature of Suit	1975	1976	1977	1978	1979	1980	Percent Change 1980 over 1979
Total.	117,320	130,597	130,567	138,770	154,666	168,789	9.1
Contracts	22,905	23,998	23,907	25,727	36,898	49,052	32.9
Insurance	2,644	3,184	3,293	3,265	3,343	3,733	11.7
Marine	3,662	4,060	3,757	4,013	4,681	4,762	1.7
Miller Act.	1,037	955	1,009	971	886	799	-9.8
Negotiable instruments	2,490	2,240	2,355	2,139	2,266	4,072	79.7
Recovery of Overpayments and Enforcement of Judgments.	681	1,087	865	1,856	9,254	15,563	68.2
Other	12,391	12,472	12,628	13,483	16,468	20,123	22.2
Real property actions	6,488	8,475	8,387	12,781	11,876	11,067	-6.8
Mortgage foreclosure.	3,546	3,683	3,979	4,159	4,711	4,674	-0.8
Land condemnation	1,391	3,037	2,801	7,021	5,599	4,763	-14.9
Other	1,551	1,755	1,607	1,601	1,566	1,630	4.1
Tort actions.	25,691	25,736	26,029	26,375	28,901	32,539	12.6
Employers' Liability Act	1,243	1,329	1,306	1,494	1,540	1,990	29.2
Marine	5,410	5,170	5,056	4,843	4,905	5,006	2.1
Motor vehicle	6,794	6,068	6,036	5,839	5,991	6,321	5.5
Other personal injury	7,774	8,635	9,067	9,770	11,520	14,200	23.3
Property damage.	4,470	4,534	4,564	4,429	4,945	5,022	1.6
Actions under statutes	60,051	70,372	70,694	73,034	76,067	75,574	-0.6
Antitrust	1,431	1,555	1,658	1,477	1,284	1,496	16.5
Civil rights	10,392	12,329	13,113	12,829	13,168	12,944	-1.7
Commerce (ICC rates, etc.)	4,042	4,396	2,549	2,365	1,395	1,105	-20.8
Deportations.	386	291	292	163	141	139	-1.4
Forfeiture and penalty suits	2,446	2,587	2,854	2,988	2,779	3,019	8.6
Labor laws	6,617	7,743	7,739	7,461	8,404	8,640	2.8
Narcotic Addict Rehabilitation Act	276	150	113	74	8	–	–
Patent, copyright, trademark	2,276	2,632	3,071	3,265	3,374	3,783	12.1
Prisoner petitions:							
Federal.	5,047	4,780	4,691	4,955	4,499	3,713	-17.5
State	14,260	15,029	14,846	16,969	18,502	19,574	5.8
Securities, commodities and exchange	2,408	2,230	1,960	1,703	1,589	1,694	6.6
Social Security laws.	5,846	10,355	10,095	9,950	9,942	9,043	-9.0
Tax suits.	1,699	1,849	1,981	2,669	3,519	3,271	-7.0
Freedom of Information Act.	*–	*–	**142	532	627	627	–
Other	2,925	4,446	5,732	6,167	6,836	6,526	-4.5
Other Actions	2,185	2,016	1,550	852	924	557	-39.7
Domestic relations (local jurisdiction)	1,130	1,186	729	304	269	94	-65.1
Insanity (local jurisdiction).	40	18	77	101	116	123	6.0
Other	1,015	812	744	447	539	340	-36.9

    * Not separately classified until March 1977.

    ** Data covers period from March - June 1977 only.

Source: Administrative Office of U.S. Courts.

Antitrust and Products Liability Cases

The two litigation examples given below in Parts II and III involve product liability and antitrust actions, respectively. The former involves a case in federal court on the basis of diversity jurisdiction; the latter an example of federal question jurisdiction.

Antitrust cases filed in federal court in fiscal 1980 totaled 1496, an increase of 16.5 percent over 1979 (see Fig. 2, p. 11). Also, indicative of the Justice Department's efforts to crack down on white-collar crime, there were more criminal antitrust cases filed in 1980 — 39 — than in any year since 1959 when there were 42 such filings (this is not shown in Fig. 2, which gives only civil case filings).

The antitrust area of federal litigation deserves special attention not only for the actual number of cases filed, but also for the overall impact these cases generally have on the federal court system. Antitrust cases are often of a complex nature and impose a relatively greater burden on court time and resources than other kinds of litigation. For example, the median time from the filing of an antitrust case in federal court to disposition (by decision, settlement, or otherwise) is 19 months. The median time for civil filings in general is eight months. It is not uncommon for antitrust cases to drag on for years.

Also, antitrust litigation is extremely important to the business community, both those cases filed by the Federal Government (the Justice Department) and those filed by private parties. Such cases play a significant role in how industries and individual companies relate to one another and the marketing and pricing practices they follow.

Products liability cases filed in federal courts are also increasing, and at a very rapid pace. In fiscal 1980, 14,200 such cases were filed in federal district courts, nationwide, an increase of 23.3 percent over the previous year. In the past six years, products liability actions filed in federal court have doubled.

While most products liability cases are filed in state courts around the country, more and more of the major products actions are being heard in federal court. More on this in Part II below.

Federal Judges

The Omnibus Judgeship Act of 1978 created 117 new federal district judges and 35 circuit judgeships for the Courts of Appeals, the largest single increase in the size of the federal court system in American history. That brings the total to 516 authorized district court judgeships and 132 authorized appeals court judgeships. As a result of the increase in federal district judges, the number of civil cases filed per judgeship dropped from 348 cases in 1978 to 300 in 1979.

More relevant, however, than the new caseload statistics is the generally acknowledged fact that civil litigation is becoming more and more complex, both in terms of the issues presented and the number of parties involved. Cases in federal court can drag on for years as judges and juries grapple with complex questions of economics and technology.

In products liability actions, for example, the courts must examine closely the design of the product under question and determine whether the alleged injury is the proximate result of a specific defect. In antitrust actions courts must deal with market structure issues, including the definition of relevant product and geographic markets and the level of market concentration among the leading firms in an industry.

Beyond their numbers and complexity, federal cases may sometimes impose a continuing burden on a court's time and resources, such as when it must exercise supervisory authority over prisons and school systems. And in class actions, the courts must steward the interests of huge numbers of persons, many of whom are not even aware that such litigation exists. (More on class actions below.)

Judicial Selection Process

Selection of federal judges — for the U.S. Supreme Court, the appeals courts, and the district courts — is with the advice and consent of the U.S. Senate. Federal judges have tenure for life during good behavior. They may retire at full salary at age 65 after 15 years service and at age 70 after 10 years. Retired judges may assume the status of "senior judge," thereby making themselves available for temporary judicial service as needed.

It is often said that life tenure serves to insure the independence of federal judges. Unlike many of their state counterparts, federal judges are not subject to periodic elections and the political pressures often associated therewith. A President, it is recognized, may choose to ignore merit selection, and appoint only those who are politically acceptable to him. Still, once appointed, a federal judge is not subject to control by either the Executive or any political leader, because he will hold office for life depending only on his own proper conduct.

Presidential nominations to federal district court judgeships have traditionally been based on recommendations of U.S. senators, particularly those belonging to the President's party. Former President Carter had attempted to restore more authority over judicial appointments with the Executive Branch, which under his plan would base nominations on the recommendation of nonpartisan panels. The panels were used for the selection of all federal appeals court judges and Democratic senators were encouraged by Carter to establish similar panels to select district court nominees. The Department of Justice reports that about half did so.

President Reagan, however, has abolished the panels set up by his predecessor and indicated his intention to restore what is known as "Senatorial Veto Power." According to the President's staff, only Republican senators will be asked to identify prospective candidates for federal district judgeships. If both senators in a state in which there is an opening for a district judge are Democrats, then Republican members of the Congressional delegation would be asked for their suggestions. While this restores considerable patronage to Republican senators, the Reagan administration has said it is firmly committed to the principle that federal judges should be chosen on the basis of merit and quality.

Under the Carter Administration, more than 85 women, blacks and Hispanics were appointed to the federal bench. One survey, however, showed that Carter had named a higher percentage of members of his own party to the bench than any President in history, although this was partly the result of having a record number of judgeships to fill.

Selection of judges for the 12 federal appeals courts has been somewhat less dominated by senatorial patronage than selection of district judges, because the jurisdiction of each appeals court exceeds state boundaries. The precise means the Reagan administration intends to use in the selection of federal appeals court judges is not yet clear. But here again senators should have considerably more clout than they did under the previous administration.

President Reagan, in considering prospects for his first appointment to the U.S. Supreme Court, relied on the recommendations of an informal White House panel headed up by Attorney General William French Smith.

In selecting Sandra O'Connor to fill the Supreme Court vacancy left by retiring Justice Potter Stewart, President Reagan became the first chief executive to choose a women for that position. Reagan's early nominations to lower federal court openings have been predominately white males. Both the Supreme Court and the lower federal court nominees have come, for the most part, from conservative Republican backgrounds and are generally acknowledged to be well qualified for the federal bench.

Special Courts

In addition to the principal courts of the federal system — the U.S. Supreme Court, the courts of appeals, and the district courts — the Congress has from time to time created special courts to deal with particular types of cases. The major special courts are: the U.S. Court of Claims, the U.S. Court of Customs and Patent Appeals, the Court of International Trade, the U.S. International Trade Commission, the Tax Court, the Judicial Panel on Multidistrict Litigation, the Temporary Court of Emergency Appeals and the U.S. Court of Military Appeals. Administrative Law Judges, who preside over federal agency hearings, will be taken up in the next section.

(1) The U.S. Court of Claims has been called the "keeper of the nation's conscience." It is generally here, as opposed to the federal district courts, that an individual citizen or corporation may sue the Federal Government for money damages in a wide variety of claims for which Congress has waived sovereign immunity.[1] Aliens and their governments may also bring suits in the U.S. Court of Claims provided their courts give our citizens the same privilege.

The Federal Government is the nation's largest contractor, purchaser and employer, and most litigation in the Court of Claims concerns these activities. The typical case is one involving complicated issues and large amounts of money. There is no monetary ceiling on the court's jurisdiction. Suits against the Government for money damages must be tried in the Court of Claims if the amount exceeds $10,000, except in tax refund claims (see below) where the

---

[1] Sovereign immunity is the doctrine that precludes suits against federal and state governments unless such governments (i.e., the sovereign) consents to be sued. The doctrine has been limited in recent years by court decision and statutory enactment, and in some states has been abolished altogether.

district courts have concurrent jurisdiction, and in tort claims where district courts have exclusive jurisdiction. If the amount is less than $10,000, the case must be heard by a U.S. district court. The Court of Claims may exercise appellate jurisdiction over the district courts in tort cases by agreement of the parties.

Citizens who pay federal taxes under formal protest may sue in the Court of Claims for refunds with interest. Also, citizens may bring suits for damages for the taking of private property for public use without just compensation in violation of the Fifth Amendment. Constitutional and statutory rights are constantly in issue in the Court of Claims, often involving personnel of the military services, active and retired, and their dependents. Civil service employees seek back pay in the Court of Claims for alleged illegal dismissal from office. Contractors sue for breach of contract. Oyster growers seek compensation for damages to their beds by dredging operations by the Corps of Engineers for harbor or channel improvement. Farmers have sued in the Court of Claims, charging the Corps with building structures in rivers that allegedly cause floods on their lands. This court is the only one where inventors can claim patent infringement against the U.S. Government. Private party actions for patent infringement are brought in U.S. district court.

The Court of Claims is a busy court with a large number of decisions handed down annually.

(2) The Court of Customs and Patent Appeals (CCPA) includes appeals from a number of quasi-judicial bodies, including among others, the U.S. Customs Court (now known as the Court of International Trade), the U.S. International Trade Commission, and the U.S. Patent and Trademark Office (PTO). The last, the PTO, provides the CCPA with the bulk of its case load. Concerning a PTO decision, a party has an election: he may appeal to the CCPA or he may ask for a new trial in federal district court. Appeals from the CCPA are directly to the U.S. Supreme Court.

(3) A recent organizational change has involved the creation in 1980 of a new court — the Court of International Trade. This court, located in New York City, has a wider jurisdiction than its forerunner, the U.S. Customs Court. The Court of International Trade has exclusive jurisdiction over conflicts arising under the Tariff Act of 1930, the Trade Act of 1974, and the Trade Agreements of 1979. Under this court, questions affecting importations will be subject to the same standard of judicial review and remedies as Congress has provided for persons aggrieved by other agency actions. The Court of International Trade also hears appeals from the U.S. International Trade Commission concerning antidumping determinations.

(4) The International Trade Commission (previously known as the Tariff Commission), in addition to its antidumping authority, investigates unfair practices in import trade. It is authorized to order that articles be excluded from entry into the United States and to issue cease and desist orders. Appeals from unfair practice determinations are to the CCPA.

(5) The Tax Court adjudicates controversies involving deficiencies or overpayments in income, estate, and gift taxes and personal holding company surtaxes. The Pension Reform Act of 1974 conferred jurisdiction on the Tax

Court to render declaratory judgments with respect to the qualification of pension and profit sharing plans. Decisions of the Tax Court, except for summary opinions issued in small tax cases, are subject to review by federal appellate courts and the U.S. Supreme Court.

A taxpayer, upon receiving a notice of deficiency in tax from the Commissioner of Internal Revenue, has a choice of three federal courts in which he can obtain a judicial determination of his rights. He may pay the tax and file a claim with the IRS for a refund. If the claim is disallowed, he may then file suit for refund in a U.S. district court or the U.S. Court of Claims, both courts having concurrent jurisdiction over such suits. If he does not wish to pay the tax beforehand, he may litigate the matter in Tax Court.

The strategy to follow depends on a number of considerations, particularly on the amount of money and issues in dispute. One advantage of using the Tax Court is that the amount in dispute need not be paid until the case is lost. Another is the simplified, inexpensive process available under the court's small-tax-case procedure. A disadvantage is that verdicts under the small-case procedure may not be appealed. And if the taxpayer loses a Tax Court case, he pays not only the additional tax but also interest accruing at 12 percent a year while the case is being litigated.

The statistics in regard to taxpayer apeals are not too encouraging. Of the 1,280 opinions rendered by Tax Court judges in 1979, only ten percent sided entirely with the taxpayer. About 53% went entirely for the Government and 37% showed mixed results. If the amount in dispute is paid, the taxpayer, as indicated, can appeal to either the Court of Claims or to a U.S. district court. The latter offers the possibility of a jury trial, through such litigation is often time-consuming and expensive.

Tax Court judges periodically travel to more than 100 cities across the country to hear taxpayer appeals.

(6) The Judicial Panel on Multidistict Litigation is a national court with a specific and important role to play in federal court litigation. The Judicial Panel, which consists of seven federal judges appointed by the Chief Justice of the U.S. Supreme Court, is authorized to temporarily transfer to a single district court, civil actions pending in different districts that involve one or more common question of fact.

The purpose of the judicial panel is to streamline the pretrial process by eliminating duplication in discovery and otherwise reducing the costs of litigation. Once pretrial proceedings are completed in the consolidated action, the cases are then transferred back to their original courts for final disposition. There are several hundred cases currently pending that have been so consolidated by the panel.

Typical subject-matter areas of cases consolidated by the judicial panel include antitrust, securities, air disaster, patent, and products liability. An example of the last is the litigation involving the Dalkon Shield intrauterine device, where hundreds of lawsuits have been filed in U.S. district courts around the country alleging injury through use of the device. Most of these cases have been transferred by the judicial panel to one district court for pretrial proceedings.[1]

(7) The Temporary Emergency Court of Appeals has exclusive jurisdiction of all appeals from U.S. district courts in cases arising under the Emergency Petroleum Allocation Act. Appeals from decisions of this court are directly to the Supreme Court.

The deregulation of the oil industry currently taking place will significantly cut down district court litigation on oil pricing and related matters and thus greatly reduce, if not take away all together, the kind of cases heard by this court.

(8) U.S. Court of Military Appeals. This court is the final appellate tribunal to review court-martial convictions of all the military services. The court consists of three civilian judges appointed by the President. In all of its cases, the decisions of the court are final — there is no further direct review.

Administrative Law Judges

In addition to the judges of the three-tiered federal judiciary and the special courts, there are the Administrative Law Judges (ALJs). Unlike the judges of the federal judiciary system who are appointed for life, ALJs are employees of the Government, more specifically the executive departments and independent agencies for whom they conduct hearings and make decisions in proceedings based on records of trial-type hearings.

When compared with the role of federal court judges, that of the ALJs is considerably less visible — ALJs have been referred to as the "Invisible Judiciary" — though not necessarily less important. A listing of some of the matters acted on by ALJs indicates the important role they play: Compliance with federal standards relating to interstate trade, labor-management relations, advertising, communications, consumer products, food and drugs, banking, corporate mergers, and antitrust; regulations of health and safety in transportation, mining, and industry; regulation of trading in securities, commodities, and futures; adjudication of claims relating to social security benefits, workers' compensation, and international trade; and many other matters.

There are approximately 1,150 ALJs employed by 29 federal agencies, twice the number of federal district court judges.

The position of administrative law judge was established by the Administrative Procedure Act, enacted in 1946. The basic intention was to provide for the objectivity and judicial capability of presiding officers in formal administrative proceedings. For example, the Act stipulates that the ALJ, though a government employee, may not be subject to supervision by anyone performing investigative or prosecutorial functions for an agency. This "separation of functions" requirement is intended to prevent the investigative arm of an agency from controlling a hearing or influencing the ALJ.

Hearings before an ALJ are quasi-judicial in nature. That is, some but not all of the formalities involved in federal court litigation apply to an administrative hearing and determination. There is, for instance, no trial by jury in an administrative hearing; the ALJ hears the case alone.

---

[1]In re Dalkon Shield IUD Litigation. Multidistrict Litigation No. 211 (District Court for Kansas).

The ruling of the ALJ may be appealed to the full agency. For example, the ruling of an ALJ for the Federal Trade Commission could be appealed to the commissioners of the FTC. Appeal from an agency decision (in the FTC example, a decision of the commissioners) generally by-passes the U.S. district court level and goes straight to the U.S. court of appeals. In 1980, appeals from decisions of federal administrative agencies constituted about 13 percent of total cases filed at the appeals court level.

PART II

FEDERAL COURT LITIGATION: A PRODUCTS LIABILITY EXAMPLE

This part and the next will examine, in simplified fashion, how a case is litigated in federal court. Here, using a products liability example, we will follow a case through its various stages of litigation. The terms and procedures described would apply generally in most state judicial systems as well. The next part (beginning on page 37) goes over similar ground using an antitrust example, though focusing on different aspects of the litigation process.

Litigation involving allegations of products liability has increased dramatically during the past decade. This reflects in large part the increasing complexity of products in popular use and also the increasing willingness of the courts, federal and state, to hold the manufacturer liable for the defective design or operation of his product. Many manufacturers argue that this litigation has reached crisis proportions, forcing them to raise prices to cover escalating insurance costs and to delay the introduction of potentially useful items for consumer use. Attorneys representing plaintiffs in products liability actions, on the other hand, see themselves as assisting their clients in receiving just compensation for the injuries they have suffered.

Most products liability actions are filed in state courts and, though no overall statistics are available, these cases appear to have been increasing rapidly in recent years. At the federal level, where statistics are available, this rapid increase is clearly seen. In fiscal 1980, 14,200 products liability cases were brought in federal courts, nationwide, an increase of 23.3 percent over 1979. During the past six years, such litigation has doubled.

The products liability suits litigated in federal court tend to be major ones, often involving popular products with nationwide distribution. It is not unusual for the (allegedly) injured plaintiff to bring his action originally in the court system of the state in which he resides — where he typically feels he can receive the most sympathetic hearing — and for the defendant, usually an out-of-state manufacturing company, to remove the case to federal court on the basis of diversity jurisdiction. Since there is no federal law as such governing products liability (as opposed to antitrust law which will be discussed below), the only way in which a federal court may hear a products liability case is on the basis of diversity, i.e., the plaintiff and defendant coming from different states. For further discussion of this subject, see section in Part I above entitled "Diversity Jurisdiction."

Examples of major products liability cases being heard in federal courts include actions involving: the Dalkon Shield intrauterine device; the Firestone multi-piece rim assembly; the aortic heart valve; and asbestos litigation, to name a few. A listing of other recently-filed products liability actions is given in Appendix II.

Products Liability Law

In products liability cases, liability for injury the plaintiff has suffered (if such is proved) may be based on one or a combination of legal theories, including: negligence in the design and manufacture of the product (including duty to warn of inherent dangers), breach of warranty, and strict liability in tort. Strict liability refers to "liability without fault." That is, the plaintiff need not go through a detailed proof of negligence or breach of warranty; all he need do in such a situation is show that the product is an unreasonably dangerous one and is in some way defective. A situation in which strict liability might apply is the case of a drug that can only be taken in limited dosages, and the manufacturer fails to warn of such.

The first prerequisite of liability in any products liability action is proof by the plaintiff that the product in question was defective or dangerous in some way. The second prerequisite is proof that his injury was "proximately" caused by the product in question. This causal connection need not be proved with absolute certainty or to the exclusion of every other possible cause but, as in any civil action, by a preponderance of the evidence. To illustrate: there have been literally thousands of suits brought in federal and state courts alleging injury as a result of exposure in the home and workplace to asbestos products. While courts have awarded damages where massive exposure could be shown, they generally have not found in favor of plaintiffs who could show only indirect exposure, or who engaged in other activities, such as cigarette smoking, which also could account for their illness or injury.

Once the plaintiff has satisfied the court as to the prerequisites to establishing liability on the part of the defendant-manufacturer, the question of damages is then considered. These monetary damages to which the plaintiff may be entitled are compensatory damages and/or punitive damages. Compensatory damages are intended to do just that — compensate the plaintiff for the injuries he has suffered, putting him in the same financial position he was prior to the injury. The phrase "actual damages" it is sometimes used as synonymous with compensatory damages.

In setting out his compensatory claim, the plaintiff should include all damages resulting from his injury, including those likely to accrue in the future. Damages in products liability actions typically include personal injuries, such as medical expenses and impaired earnings, and damage to property, i.e., home or business. If business losses are claimed, compensatory damages would include economic loss, such as replacement cost of the product and lost business income.

Punitive damages (sometimes known as "exemplary damages") may also be awarded by the court. Punitive damages in a products liability action are intended to punish a manufacturer who markets a product with a known defect or who recklessly disregards the safety of the consumer by marketing the product without proper testing. To illustrate, punitive damages of one million dollars were recently assessed against a textile company for manufacturing highly flammable childrens' pajamas.[1] Also, in a case stemming from the fiery crash of a Ford Pinto, a California state appeals court affirmed a jury award of three million dollars in compensatory damages and three and a half million in

---

[1] *Grye v. Dayton-Hudson Corp.,* Minn SupCt (1980).

punitive damages. The jury had found that the Pinto was unsafe, particularly in regard to the placement of its fuel tank.

Steps of Civil Litigation Process

Let us now run through the steps involved in litigating a civil case in federal district court, using a products liability case as an example.[1] For our example, suppose that a person was severely lacerated by the blade of his lawnmower while he was using it, so he contends, under normal conditions. He brings suit in federal court against the manufacturer of the lawnmower, alleging negligence in design of the mower (including failure to warn of dangers involved in its operation) and breach of warranty. He could, of course, have brought the action in state court; but we will assume diversity applies (i.e., the defendant-manufacturer is from out-of-state) and plaintiff on his own initiative has chosen a federal forum.

The plaintiff begins by filing a "complaint", which is the formal written statement in which the plaintiff presents the facts as he believes them to be, and demands the relief to which he believes he is entitled. (See "Glossary of Terms," Appendix I.) In a products liability action, as indicated, a person may recover compensatory damages in essentially three areas: (1) for personal injuries, including both compensation for bodily harm and emotional distress; (2) for property damages, which encompass damages to one's property including the defective product; and (3) for economic loss (if such applies), which includes compensation for loss of the value or use of the defective product itself as well as damages for harm to the person's business.

The defendant is now required to file an "answer" to the complaint. The answer is the defendant's version of what happened. Generally, he will deny all or part of what the plaintiff has claimed.

The plaintiff and defendant are the "parties" to the suit; they are called opposing parties or adversaries because they are taking positions contrary to one another. They are sometimes called "litigants" and the proceedings in court, the "litigation."

There is a special procedure — called a summons — for notifying a person that he is being sued and that he must file an answer within a given time. A "summons" is a "writ," a formal command from the court. It is served by the federal marshal notifying the person named in the suit that a complaint has been filed against him and that he is required to appear in court to answer that complaint. This is known as "service of process."

The summons joins the parties and begins the litigation process. When the papers have been served, the marshal makes a "return" to the court. Reporting back to the court, the marshal gives an account of his actions under the writ — the time and manner of service or the reason why he was unable to serve it, if that was the case.

The complaint and the answer make up the "pleadings," the formal allega-

---

[1]The discussion given in this section and the two that follow are based in part on material prepared by the Administrative Office of the U.S. Courts.

tions of the parties regarding their respective claims and defenses. From these pleadings it is possible to determine the general nature of the dispute. The specifics will come later, in memoranda of facts and law (see, e.g., Appendix IV), discovery documents, and other material filed as the litigation progresses.

Once the answer is filed, the "issues have been joined," meaning that the parties have agreed to the basic questions constituting the dispute. It is not uncommon for lawsuits to be settled at this early point in the action, particularly if one party after studying the pleadings, views his case as a weak one or otherwise in his interest to settle. If the action is not settled, it moves to the pretrial stage.

Pretrial

The pretrial phase of the litigation begins the important "discovery" process. This refers to the process through which the parties obtain from each other and from other sources the information necessary to support their respective positions. The plaintiff, for instance, would want information from the defendant-manufacturer on similar consumer complaints involving the product in question and data from the company's engineers on product safety tests. The manufacturer, on the other hand, would seek to elicit from the plaintiff the facts surrounding the alleged accident and the manner in which the plaintiff claims it occurred. The manufacturer, of course, is interested in whether the plaintiff was using the product in an unsafe manner or manner in which it was not intended to be used. The defendant also would want to know the specific parts of the product claimed to be defective.

The popular view of the trial attorney is that of someone cross-examining a hostile witness or making an impassioned closing argument before a spellbound jury. This is not an accurate view of the workaday world of the typical trial attorney. In truth, such attorneys spend much of their professional careers in discovery — that is, examining documents, taking depositions, and drafting and responding to interrogatories (these terms are discussed below).

The Federal Rules of Civil Procedure, which is followed by all federal courts, provides for liberal discovery of information. The theory for this is that with each side knowing the strength of its case, early settlements will be encouraged and the time and expense of a trial avoided. While such is often the case — over 90 percent of civil actions filed in federal court are in fact settled prior to trial —discovery can be used as a delaying tactic also. This is discussed in the antitrust litigation example in Part III.

Interrogatories, the most frequently used discovery device in products liability cases, are written questions served on an opponent, who then is required to provide written answers under oath.

An oral statement made under oath before an officer of the court and taken down in writing, usually by a court reporter, is called a "deposition." The attorney for the opposing party is notified to attend the deposition and may cross-examine the deposed party. Anyone may be deposed, whether they are parties to the suit, witnesses, etc. The deposition is generally used for obtaining background information, but under certain conditions (such as unavailability of witnesses), it may also be introduced in evidence at the trial.

A "motion" is an application to the Court for an order, ruling, or the like. A "motion to compel production of documents" is a request made to the court when one party knows or has reason to believe that the opposing party has in his possession some document such as a statement made by a witness at the time of the accident, or (as per our lawn mower example) a report describing similar rotating blade injuries. If the court decides that he is entitled to see them, the judge will order them produced. All motions are made by counsel (attorneys) for the parties involved in the lawsuit.

There is no limit to the number of requests that can be asked for by motion. Before the day of trial arrives, the parties may have made any or all of the following motions.

A "motion to amend the complaint" is a request asking the court's permission to correct an error in the complaint or to add additional information.

A "motion to dismiss" is a request to dismiss the case altogether. For example, the defendant may allege that the court does not have jurisdiction over him, or that there is no legal basis to grant relief.

A "motion for judgement on the pleadings" is a request which can be made and granted if the pleadings alone (i.e. the complaint and answer) show that one party is entitled to a judgment without the necessity of a trial or additional showing to the court. Judges are often reluctant to grant this motion on the premise that parties deserve their day in court.

A "motion for change of venue" is a request made by the defendant who wishes to have his case transferred to a more convenient location. The court will weigh the problems and convenience of both parties and decide which forum is most appropriate.

A "motion to extend time" is a request for an extension of time to complete some phase of the proceedings. The defendant, for example, is required to answer the complaint within 20 days, but the court, for good cause, may extend this time.

The defendant-manufacturer (in our products liability example) may know that his product was defective and did cause the injury complained of, but that the defect was the result of the negligence of a subassembly supplier under contract to the manufacturer. He, therefore, sues that supplier who becomes the "third party defendant." The supplier is a third party to the suit — an outsider brought in as a defendant.

After discovery has gone on for a period, the judge may call a "pretrial conference." This is a somewhat informal meeting between the attorneys for both sides with the judge acting as moderator. At the pretrial conference, the judge attempts to narrow the issues as much as possible and encourage the parties to settle the case before trial.

Trial

If the parties cannot reach a settlement, the case will be set for trial. In a product liability case, the parties are entitled to trial by jury. If neither party so requests, the case will be heard and decided by a judge sitting without a jury.

The "jury trial" is basically a proceeding in which each side presents the case to a group of disinterested, impartial, and qualified persons.[1] The judge supervises and rules upon many questions that come up during the trial and instructs the jury in the law to be applied to the facts as presented.

The jurors are selected from the "jury venire," which is a panel made up of persons selected at random who have been ordered into court to serve as jurors. From the jury venire, six or more persons will be selected to try the case. (Criminal cases still require a twelve member jury in the federal courts. The size of the civil jury is determined by the local rules of the particular federal district.) The judge will ask each juror his name, occupation, and other questions to determine whether he is impartial, or prejudiced in favor of or against either party. This questioning is called a "voir dire" examination. If one of the prospective jurors is a relative or close friend of one of the parties, that person obviously could not be considered disinterested and impartial, and should not serve on the jury. The opposing party is entitled to "challenge" any prospective juror who he has reason to believe is other than disinterested and impartial. This is called a "challenge for cause." The judge rules on whether or not there is sufficient reason to exclude this person from the jury. If the judge decides there is sufficient reason, that person is excused and another called in his place. Each side is also allowed a limited number of "peremptory challenges." By use of the peremptory challenge, a person may be excluded from the jury without the need for the attorney to identify a particular reason.

At this point, we should distinguish between a "petit jury" and a "grand jury." The petit jury is the type presently under discussion. This jury hears a case, whether civil or criminal, and renders a verdict. A grand jury, although selected in much the same manner, has a different function. Grand jurors are involved in prospective criminal cases only; they are asked to decide whether there is enough evidence to cause a person to be brought to trial for a crime. They hear only the government's side of the case and do not render a verdict. Their final decision is an "indictment." An indictment is merely an accusation, a decision that the person in question should stand trial to determine his innocence or guilt.

In our product liability case, which is a civil action being heard by a petit jury, the plaintiff must prove that the defendant is responsible for plaintiff's injury and should pay damages for the injury he has suffered. The plaintiff has the "burden of proof." It is not sufficient for him to explain to the jury why he *thinks* he is right. He must prove it by presenting "evidence." This is accomplished by offering into evidence relevant documents and by calling witnesses, such as persons who may have seen the accident and experts to testify as to design defects.

"Testimony" is the oral evidence given by the witness as distinguished from that derived from writings and other documents.

The defendant then has the task of rebutting the proof offered by the plaintiff.

---

[1]There is always a right to a trial by jury in a criminal case. In a civil suit, however, that right is not absolute; it depends on several considerations, including whether the case is one at "common law" (as our example here), as opposed to one based on statutory enactment. In the latter case, the right to trial by jury generally depends on whether the statute specifically so provides.

He may attempt to "impeach" one or more of the plaintiff's witnesses or to present other witnesses whose testimony may contradict them. To impeach a witness is to discredit him, to induce the jury not to believe him, because he is not truthful or, as is sometimes the case with expert witnesses, lacks proper credentials in his field.

The attorney presents the testimony of a witness by means of "direct examination." He asks questions, the answers to which are likely to bring out the facts he wants to establish. After the examination, the opposing attorney "cross-examines" the witness by asking questions designed to test the truth of his testimony or to bring out other relevant facts.

Witnesses to an accident may be unable or not want to take a day away from their work to come into court to testify. The attendance of witnesses at trial is secured by means of a "subpoena." A subpoena is a command that a person appear in court for the purpose of giving testimony. It is issued by the clerk under the seal of the court and served by the marshal or any adult not a party to the suit.

A "subpoena duces tecum" commands a person to appear in court to testify and also to bring certain books or records which he has in his possession. A subpoena duces tecum might be issued to the defendant company's engineer in charge of production, commanding that he bring in background reports and safety data in connection with the allegedly defective product.

The jury considers the evidence as presented, including the arguments of the attorneys. The judge then "charges" the jury by instructing them on the law as it is to be applied to the facts as presented in the case. The jury retires to consider what they have heard and discuss the issues among themselves. This is called "deliberation." They then agree among themselves on a "verdict" which is their formal decision.

If the jury cannot agree on a verdict — this is known as a "hung" jury — a mistrial is declared and the judge may order that the case be tried again. In actual practice, retrial of cases is rare. Plaintiffs' attorneys in civil cases and prosecutors in criminal cases are generally reluctant to push for a retrial. They say that attorneys for the defense tend to learn more from the first trial than they do. A retrial, when it does occur, may result not only from a hung jury but also by a reversal and remand by a higher court, such as when an appeals court says the trial court judge incorrectly instructed the jury and that the case must therefore be tried again.

In an evaluation of jury instructions, a recent study sponsored by the Department of Justice concluded that the instructions were often not fully understood by the average juror. The study was undertaken in an attempt to determine the impact that often complex legal requirements, as explained by the judge in his instructions, have on the decision making of a jury. The study found that the average juror may understand no more than half of a judge's instructions on the law to be applied in a particular case. Among other recommendations, the study said that common language should be used in jury instructions and that jurors should be allowed to take written instructions with them when deliberations begin.

If the case has been tried by the court (i.e., tried by the judge without a jury), the judge makes findings of fact *and* conclusions of law. In either event, the final step is the "entry of the court's judgment." This is the final order of the court and states the rights and obligations of each of the parties to the suit.

If the case has been tried by a jury, after the jury has returned its verdict, either party may, if he feels that the verdict is obviously wrong, make a "motion for judgment N.O.V.," i.e., "judgment notwithstanding the verdict." This motion requests the court to render a judgment different from the jury's verdict. It can be granted only if, in the opinion of the presiding judge, the evidence introduced at the trial fails to support the verdict of the jury.

Also, a party may feel that the trial was grossly unfair and he may make a "motion for a new trial." If this motion is granted, the entire trial process is repeated, beginning with the selection of a new jury.

If either party, however, believes that an error occurs during the course of the trial, there is no need to wait until the end of the trial to make a motion for a new trial. At the time of the indiscretion, either party may call it to the attention of the court with a request to declare a "mistrial." If such request is granted, the trial is immediately stopped, the jurors excused, and a completely new trial scheduled for a later date.

At the end of the trial, the judgment is entered. If the plaintiff has prevailed, he has obtained a judgment entitling him to recover from the defendant a certain amount of money. This judgment typically represents the value in dollars of the damage he has suffered from the accident. Generally, he will also be awarded interest and "costs," which, like the assessed damages, are the responsibility of the losing party. The costs awarded are the expenses of the trial, such as the witness fees and mileage which were paid at the time the witnesses were subpoenaed, and the expenses involved in taking depositions.

The attorney fees, which are usually the biggest expense the parties bear in a trial, typically are not included in the costs which the losing party must pay. That is, the general rule is that each party must pay its own attorneys' fees, regardless of who wins or loses. Most products liability cases, however, are taken on a contingency fee basis. That is, if the plaintiff prevails at trial (or on the basis of a settlement prior to trial), the plaintiff's attorney gets a certain percentage of the amount so obtained, generally one-third. If, on the other hand, the defendant prevails, the plaintiff's attorney receives nothing in attorneys fees.

Because of this contingency fee arrangement, the attorney for the plaintiff in such a case plays a role similar to that of an entrepreneur. In taking the (products liability) case, he accepts the risk that he may receive no compensation for his efforts or he may be rewarded handsomely, depending on the outcome of the case. Needless to say, such a lawyer-entrepreneur would not survive very long unless he achieved some success in the courtroom or at the settlement table.

Appeal of Verdict

If either (or both) parties are dissatisfied with the verdict, he may file a "notice of appeal." This notifies the parties concerned that the case is not over. If the defendant is appealing a judgment ordering him to pay the plaintiff, he may obtain a "stay of execution" by giving a "supersedeas bond." This stay of execution will prevent the plaintiff from collecting the judgment until the case has been reviewed on appeal, by the appropriate U.S. Court of Appeals. The supersedeas bond must be of sufficient amount to ensure that the judgment will be paid if and when it becomes due.

The "appellant" is the party that brings the appeal; the "appellee" is the party against whom the appeal is brought. If the manufacturer, who is the defendant in our products liability example, loses the case and decides to appeal, he would be the appellant. The injured party who won the verdict, who was the plaintiff in the original action, would be the appellee.

The Court of Appeals does not try the case again, but "reviews" the case from the record. The entire "original record" — all the papers and exhibits filed in the case during the federal district court proceedings — is forwarded to the Court of Appeals hearing the case. This court, generally consisting of a panel of three judges, will study the record and consider the objections or alleged errors. The attorneys for each side will submit a printed "brief," which is a written presentation to the court explaining his position and citing authorities that support it. The attorneys may be allowed to present oral arguments as well, if the court considers it necessary.

The Court of Appeals will render a decision either "affirming" the judgment of the district court (i.e., agreeing with the lower court) or "reversing" it (i.e., the judgment is ordered changed). If the judgment is reversed, the case may also be "remanded," that is, sent back to the district court for the taking of further evidence or some other action as specified by the appeals court.

If the parties are dissatisfied with the decision of the federal Court of Appeals, they may seek review by the U.S. Supreme Court. They petition for Supreme Court review through a "writ of certiorari" (see section in Part I above entitled "Three-Tiered Court System"). If certiorari is denied, then the appeals court judgment stands.

Criminal Procedure

Our products liability illustration and the antitrust case to follow in Part III exemplify the litigation of civil lawsuits. A criminal case proceeds along the same lines, although there are a number of aspects in which criminal cases differ and instances in which different terms are used.

For a criminal case to be tried in federal court, there must, of course, be a violation of federal law. There are federal criminal laws, for example, relating to such offenses as drug usage, mail fraud, and tax evasion. Federal antitrust law (which will be discussed further below) provides for both civil *and* criminal actions.

If it appears that there is a probable cause to believe that someone has violated a federal criminal statute, a "warrant for arrest" is issued by the federal magistrate. The warrant names the defendant, describes the crime, and orders the marshal to arrest him. The magistrate may, at the request of the U.S. Attorney, issue a "summons," which orders the defendant to appear before the magistrate at a stated time and place, rather than having him arrested and brought before the court.

The U.S. marshal or other person making the arrest must bring the defendant before the magistrate without unnecessary delay, at which time the defendant is informed of his rights and a bail hearing is held. He is not yet called upon to plead innocent or guilty. At this point, he may "retain counsel" (i.e., call in his own attorney whom he will pay himself) or, if he cannot afford to provide adequately for his own defense, have counsel appointed for him at government expense under the Criminal Justice Act. Most states, through their public defender programs, provide similar services for persons charged with violation of state criminal law.

Bail is an amount of money or other things of value that may be deposited or guaranteed to assure that the defendant will be present at the time set for trial. A "surety bond" is a commitment to pay a certain amount of money if the conditions of the bail bond are not met. If the defendant does not appear for trial the bond is forfeited. Bonds may be executed by a commercial bonding company or by a private individual who owns sufficient property to satisfy the amount promised. In the case of corporate surety bonds, there are regulations of the Treasury Department governing the acceptability of these bonds, and only those that meet the requirements may be accepted by the court to procure the defendant's release pending trial.

In 1966, Congress enacted the Bail Reform Act, which provided for pretrial release of persons accused of non-capital crimes. The intention was to end pretrial imprisonment of certain indigent defendants who could not afford to post money bail. The Act also discouraged the traditional use of money bail by requiring federal judges to seek other means likely to insure that defendants would appear when their trials were held.

If no charges have been filed against the defendant, he is entitled to a "preliminary examination" at which evidence is presented. If the evidence does not indicate that there is probable cause to believe the defendant has committed a crime, he is discharged and the papers in the proceedings are forwarded to the clerk for termination of the case. If there appears to be probable cause, the defendant is then held to answer the complaint in the district court.

The formal accusation charging the defendant with the commission of a crime is known as the "indictment" and is brought by the grand jury. The grand jurors, summoned to hear the evidence presented to them by the prosecution may subpoena witnesses and gather additional information. The grand jury does not determine the innocence or guilt of the accused, and it usually does not hear his side of the story. It merely decides whether there is enough evidence to cause him to be tried. If it decides that the evidence is sufficient, the grand jury returns an indictment. The indictment states the facts constituting the crime and cites the particular law which the defendant is alleged to have violated.

Not every criminal accusation need be brought by way of an indictment. Prosecutions of less serious offenses may be initiated by an "information." An information is a formal accusation filed by the U.S. Attorney. Defendants in felony cases may also waive indictment and agree to be prosecuted on an information.

The next step in the criminal process is the "arraignment." This is a proceeding in which the defendant is called into open court, the indictment or information is read, and a copy is presented to him. The defendant is then required to enter his plea. He may plead: not guilty, guilty, or nolo contendere. "Nolo contendere," or no contest, means that the defendant does not admit guilt, but he generally will be sentenced by the court just as though he had pleaded or been found guilty. The judge, using his discretion, has the right to accept or reject a plea of nolo contendere. Many federal cases brought against so-called white-collar crime are disposed of in this manner.

In white-collar prosecutions, it is not uncommon for the corporation or business entity to be charged along with the officers of the organization. The corporation is subject only to the assessment of fines; the officers are subject, depending on the specific violations alleged, to both fines and incarceration.

If the defendant pleads not guilty, he is returned to custody or allowed to go free on bail while awaiting the trial date. In all criminal cases, except those punishable by death, the defendant has a right to be released on personal recognizance or upon an unsecured appearance bond, unless the court finds that such a release will not reasonably assure the reappearance of the defendant. In that case, further conditions may be imposed.

During the time before trial, depositions may be taken and witnesses subpoenaed. The rules for this are somewhat different from those in a civil case, but basically the meaning of the terms is the same.

The selection of the trial jury is also similar, but the criminal jury consists of twelve members (as opposed to a minimum of six in a civil case), and a greater number of peremptory challenges are allowed in its selection. A defendant may waive his right to trial by jury.

The jury will return a verdict of guilty or not guilty. The verdict must be unanimous, and the jury may be polled (asking each juror to verify his verdict) to assure that there is unanimous concurrence.

While the federal courts operate under rules that require 12 members and a unanimous verdict in criminal (as opposed to civil) jury trials, the Supreme Court has held that there is no Constitutional right to such requirements and that the states are free to set different standards, as long as a defendant's right to due process and a fair trial are not violated. In a Louisiana case, for instance, the Court upheld a 9/12 verdict in a criminal case.

If the defendant is found not guilty, a "judgment of acquittal" will be entered discharging him from the indictment or information by which he had been charged.

If the jury returns a verdict of guilty, a "sentence" will be imposed soon thereafter by the judge, setting the penalties to be imposed upon the convicted defendant. If the jury cannot agree on a verdict, the court will declare a mistrial, and the defendant may be subject to being tried again.

Before sentencing, the probation office must make a "presentence investigation." This investigation inquires into the defendant's family background and circumstances and reports to the court any information that may assist in imposing sentence.

Depending upon the statutory range of penalties applicable to the crime and upon the circumstances of the individual defendant, sentence may involve imprisonment, a fine and/or probation. "Probation" allows a convicted person to remain at large, usually under supervision of a probation officer, with his sentence suspended as long as he behaves lawfully and observes the conditions of probation. Probation is often granted in situations of less severe offenses or for first offenders.

Following the sentencing, a "judgment of conviction" is entered, setting forth the plea, the verdict of the jury (or finding of the court if the case was tried without a jury), and the "adjudication," the pronouncing of conviction and sentence.

As in a civil case, an appeal may be had from a judgment in a criminal action. But this is generally limited to the right of the accused to appeal his conviction. A prosecutor who fails to win a conviction cannot, in most instances, appeal the acquittal.

Federal Magistrates

In discussing the federal district courts above, mention was made of federal magistrates, the court officials who serve as assistants to U.S. district judges. Magistrates are playing an increasingly important role in the criminal and civil litigation process. They have the authority to try misdemeanor cases and, by consent of the parties, certain civil actions as well.

In civil actions, federal magistrates hear discovery motions, conduct pretrial conferences, and hold settlement conferences. Magistrates also issue reports and recommendations to the judges for disposition of a variety of other matters, principally in Social Security appeals, habeas corpus petitions brought by state prisoners, and prisoner civil rights cases.

There is a right to appeal to the district court judge from all orders issued by a magistrate. In civil actions tried by a magistrate with the consent of the parties, the appeal can lie with the district court or the circuit court as stipulated by the parties.

Before moving on to our antitrust litigation example in Part III, there are several more topics that will be taken up, including the class action lawsuit, latent disease products liability actions, million-dollar jury verdicts, and summary jury trials.

Class Actions

One of the most potent weapons available to plaintiffs in suits against large corporations is the class action lawsuit. The class action is a device allowed under the Federal Rules of Civil Procedure by which a party can sue on behalf of a large group of individuals who have claims similar to his own. In the lawnmower example given above, if the plaintiff had reason to believe that many other persons had suffered similar injury he could bring a class action in which he would serve as representative for others similarly injured. Other examples: a worker in a particular manufacturing operation who believes he suffered injury through being exposed to asbestos products may bring a lawsuit on behalf of himself and others in the plant or entire industry similarly exposed. Likewise, a retailer who purchased a product that he believes was the subject of a price-fixing agreement may bring an antitrust class action on behalf of those who were similarly injured by the alleged conspiracy.

For a suit to proceed as a class action, the presiding judge must certify it as such. Before so doing, he must determine that the members of the class do indeed have similar claims and the plaintiff who brings the action can adequately represent their interests. Once the case is certified, the litigation process as described above can proceed. Class actions may involve as few as 15 or 20 claimants, though more typically the number is in the hundreds or even the thousands. For example, the U.S. District Court for the Eastern District of New York recently certified all Vietnam War veterans, their families and survivors as potential plaintiffs in the class action suit against manufacturers of the herbicide Agent Orange, used as a defoliant in the Vietnam War.[1] It is estimated that the number of class members could reach 6,000.

Class actions have been much more prevalent in antitrust, securities, and civil rights actions than in products liability cases. Despite the vast numbers of persons injured by certain products, the principal hurdle in certifying a class in products liability cases is whether common questions of law or fact predominate over questions affecting only individual members. In the Agent Orange case mentioned above, the court did grant class action certification. But in a recent state court products liability action in which class certification was requested, the court decided otherwise. In that suit, the plaintiff commenced a class action for personal injuries allegedly caused by the defective manufacture of a cardiac pacemaker.[2] The class purportedly consisted of approximately 4,000 individuals who were required to undergo a second operation for the implantation of the pacemaker due to a defect in the first one manufactured by the defendant. In affirming the dismissal of the class action, the state appellate court found a lack of predominance of common questions of fact, since the facts demonstrated that the defendant's liability could vary from claim to claim and the activities and skills of the prescribing physicians and installing surgeons could have different degrees of relevancy.

Once class action status is denied, each claimant is free to seek legal remedy on his own behalf. The main stumbling block for most claimants, however, in pursuing an individual claim is the financial costs involved in the litigation process.

The idea behind the class action is to enable the plaintiff, who may be of limited financial means or whose injuries may not justify the costs associated with a major lawsuit, to join with others in similar circumstances. This makes a lawyer much more willing to take on such a case, which is generally brought against large corporations who can bring considerable legal muscle to bear. If the plaintiff's attorney wins the suit, or gains a favorable settlement, he will probably receive a large fee, since class judgments are generally large. If he loses, he will likely get nothing for his efforts.

The members of the class do not have to make an appearance in the case once it has been certified as a class action, but they must be notified about the case

[1]In re "Agent Orange" Product Liability Litigation.
[2]*Rose v. Medtronics Inc.* Cal App. 3d (1980).

and given a right to exclude themselves should they so desire. Members of the class have the right to approve or disapprove any proposed settlement. An individual may decide to exclude himself from membership in the class (as a class member his potential recovery would be the same as the other class members) and join the suit as a party plaintiff or file his own lawsuit separate from the class action.

An example of the huge sums of money typically involved in class action lawsuits is the $2 billion Equity Funding insurance fraud case filed in Los Angeles in 1973. In that case more than 20 law firms, acting on behalf of over 15,000 aggrieved security holders, sued the accountants, brokers, and others involved in the deal for allegedly selling stock based on fraudulent claims. In 1977, shortly before the case was set to go to trial, the defendants settled out of court for what is considered one of the biggest cash settlements on record —$62 million. The plaintiff lawyer fees amounted to $6.5 million, which figured to an average hourly legal fee of $180. The average award for each class member was $3,640.

The class action procedure has its proponents and its critics. Consumer advocates see the class action as a means through which a citizen may seek redress where otherwise no effective means may be available. Critics of the procedure, however, mainly manufacturers against whom such suits are usually directed, claim that the situation has gotten out of hand, that plaintiffs' lawyers sometimes seek out the class action suit because of the large fees they can collect if they force a settlement or prevail at trial. It recently was reported, for instance, that two Sacramento, Calif., law firms filed a class action against Piper Aircraft on the grounds that a number of crashes had been caused by defects in the fuel system of one of its aircraft. The law firms then hired a public relations agency to spread the word about the planes in order to bring more plaintiffs into the action.

The U.S. Supreme Court has in recent years tightened up somewhat on the class action procedure. And while the potential for abuse is certainly still there, a good argument can be made that class action lawsuits serve as a way of holding large corporations and governmental units responsible in some measure for the injuries they may inflict.

Latent Disease Suits

There has been an explosion in recent years of products liability actions dealing with "latent" diseases — that is, illnesses appearing several years, sometimes as many as 20 to forty years, after initial exposure to some toxic substance. Examples of such products in which a large number of claims have been filed in federal district courts around the country include: the "Agent Orange" defoliant used in Vietnam, the anti-miscarriage drug DES, and asbestos-related cases.

Experts say that latent disease suits will further flood the courts in the 1980's and possibly threaten the financial stability of some industries and insurance companies. It is expected, for instance, that diseases allegedly related to exposure to toxic materials in industrial waste dumps, such as that of the Love Canal area, may be the next major round of such actions.

Lawyers note a combination of factors in the rapid rise of latent disease suits. First, it is only in recent years that medical science has been able to identify links between toxic substances and certain diseases. This link is essential in establishing the grounds for bringing such suits in the first place. Secondly, plaintiff's lawyers in many instances have been able to gain judicial acceptance of strict liability theories in latent disease actions. Thirdly, courts often have adopted a "deep pockets" policy of basing liability not necessarily on who may have caused the injury but on who best is able to pay for it.

A related development concerns the problem of an injury being alleged but the plaintiff unable to identify the specific manufacturer. Generally in such situations, a plaintiff would be out of luck. But things may be changing. In a pioneering ruling, the California Supreme Court has recently established a theory of recovery to permit injured parties to collect even when they cannot identify the specific manufacturer of the product at issue.

The theory of recovery used by the California court is based on "market share" — defendants pay damages according to their share of the market. The case involved the drug DES, which was produced at one time or another by a number of different manufacturers. In requiring compensation based on market share rather than specific identity of the manufacturer, the ruling in effect removes the causation link between the injured party and the product manufacturer. If the California decision is followed in other states, it will considerably ease the evidentiary burden of plaintiffs in a wide range of cases involving popular consumer products.

Asbestos Cases

In terms of the number of cases filed, asbestos litigation has become the nation's largest products liability area, surpassing litigation in such areas as Agent Orange and DES. More than 25,000 asbestos cases have been filed in federal and state courts around the country and new cases are entering the system at the rate of several hundred per month.

Asbestos is a mineral highly valued for industrial uses as an insulator and fire retardant. It is widely used in such products as textiles, wall board, brake linings, floor tiles and roofing shingles. Since the early 1900's, it has been recognized that exposure to concentrated doses of asbestos dust could lead to an incapacitating lung disease called asbestosis. But it was not until the 1960's that evidence began to emerge that suggested that the mineral, even in much smaller doses, could cause asbestosis as well as cancer of the lungs and stomach. Most asbestos cases have involved workers who were directly exposed on the job. According to Johns-Manville Corp., the defendant in most of the cases filed, there has not yet been an asbestos recovery on indirect exposure, such as living in a house with asbestos insulation or using a consumer product, for example, a hair dryer, containing asbestos.

There have been to date fewer than 40 asbestos trials. Some were won by the plaintiff — jury awards have ranged from a low of $16,000 to a high of $1.1 million. In some of the asbestos trials the defendant manufacturers prevailed, generally when the plaintiff was unable to establish a direct causal link between his injury and exposure to asbestos. The vast majority of asbestos cases, however, have been settled prior to trial. Plaintiff attorneys, who generally receive contingency fees of one-third to one-half, estimate that settlements are averaging around $65,000 per claimant.

In a recent asbestos case that was being heard in the U.S. District Court for the Eastern District of Virginia, the defendants settled just prior to the date set for trial for an amount of $212,000. The case involved a suit by a woman who claimed that her husband, a pipefitter and insulator, died at age 64 as a result of the accumulation of asbestos fibers in his lungs. The woman claimed that the defendant manufacturers had failed to warn workers of the dangers of exposure to asbestos and did not take steps to properly safeguard them. The settlement was paid jointly by the 13 defendants, with Johns-Manville Corp. paying the largest share.

Defendants in asbestos cases, because of the large sums of money involved, are demanding that their insurers indemnify them for their loses. A controversial issue has arisen as to how to determine when an injury occurred, and thus which insurance companies are liable — an issue considered fundamental in insurance law, striking at the heart not only of asbestos litigation but products liability in general.

On one side of the controversy, there are those who argue that an insurance carrier should share in paying for litigation costs if the victim was exposed to the toxic substance during the time when the insurance was in effect, though coverage may subsequently have lapsed. This is referred to as the "exposure" theory of coverage. On the other side, there is the "manifestation" theory. Under this view, liability attaches when a worker first manifests the symptoms of an asbestos-related disease, typically years after exposure first occurred. The former theory spreads the risk among all insurers down the line to the time of first exposure. Proponents of the latter — the manifestation theory — argue that it makes administration of claims easier; only an insurer covering a producer when a worker first gets sick would handle the suit.

Insurance attorneys say the issue is particularly vital to Johns-Manville, the principal defendant in most of the asbestos cases, and its future financial liability. If, according to the attorneys, the courts say coverage starts on the date of discovery of the illness, the manifestation theory, then the insurer covering Johns-Manville at that time is going to lose a lot of money, and the following year be reluctant to continue covering the company, or do so only at a significantly higher rate. But if it decided that the date of exposure is spread back over a 30 or 40 year period, then the risk will be distributed among many more insurers. The courts have ruled differently on the issue, and it is one that will likely have to be decided by the U.S. Supreme Court, or perhaps by Congress.

Asbestos litigation is the first of the latent disease, products liability actions to flood the courts and will likely continue unabated in the years ahead. Experts, in fact, consider asbestos just the tip of the iceberg in potential latent disease litigation, and believe that the manner in which the courts deal with the issues raised in asbestos cases will set the tone for litigation involving many other products and companies.

Million-Dollar Verdicts

The higher the jury verdicts and settlements plaintiffs are able to obtain the greater the encouragement to bring their claims to court. The indications are that plaintiff compensation in this regard is on the increase. Mention above was made of a $1.1 million verdict in an asbestos case. A recent study reports that million-dollar verdicts are being awarded in increasing numbers.

The study, sponsored by Jury Verdict Research Inc., found that in 1979 (the latest year for which complete figures are available) there were 80 jury awards of $1 million or more, up from 66 the year before. Juries in California, Florida and New York were the most generous in the country, the study said.

In the typical $1 million verdict, according to the study, the plaintiff had suffered brain damage, was permanently paralyzed, or otherwise catastrophically injured. The usual defendant in such suits was either a manufacturer in a products liability action or a medical institution in a medical malpractice case.

The study found that the average verdict in products liability cases in 1979 —not counting million-dollar verdicts — was $225,000. Including million-dollar verdicts, the average increased to $761,000. In medical malpractice cases, the average verdict, not including million-dollar verdicts, was $218,000; including million-dollar verdicts, the average was $367,000.

Verdicts in 1979 showed an annual increase in award size of over 17 percent, the largest increase ever recorded, the study said, adding that this increase followed relatively small increases in the prior two years and parallels a substantial increase in the Consumer Price Index in 1979. The study noted, however, that when considering products liability and malpractice verdicts, one important fact is often overlooked: less than one-half of such cases tried by a jury result in a plaintiff verdict.

The study, it should be noted, dealt only with jury verdicts. It did not evaluate the amount received by a plaintiff when his case was settled, which is how the predominate number of products liability actions (and civil actions in general) are disposed of. But the best estimates are that settlement amounts are on the increase as well.

The growing sums involved in verdicts and settlements can pose difficult problems for those, particular insurance companies, ordered to pay up. In an effort to deal with this problem, a number of states now allow payments in personal injury cases to be paid on an installment basis.

Summary Jury Trials

Though most cases are settled prior to trial, those that do go to trial involve considerable legal expense and use of court resources. A test-trial procedure designed to reduce these costs and encourage out-of-court settlements is being tried with some success by several federal and state courts. This process — called a "summary jury trial" — enables parties to a lawsuit to have the benefit of a jury verdict, often in a matter of hours, rather than the weeks or months that a full-scale trial would consume. This summary procedure has been used with particular success in products liability cases.

The summary jury trial is a nonbinding procedure (the parties still have the option of a full trial) that allows attorneys to obtain a quick reading of a jury's mind. Under the summary process, each side takes one hour to present its case. No witnesses can be called, but each side is permitted to make an opening statement, submit a summary of the evidence that would be used in a full trial, and present a closing statement.

The summary jury, generally six in number, is drawn from the pool of prospective jurors for regular trials. The jury renders its decision before a judge or magistrate. The judge then asks the parties to consider the jury's findings for two weeks. If they cannot settle the case, the litigants can go ahead with a normal trial.

Move to Abolish Diversity Jurisdiction

Products liability cases in federal court are there on the basis of diversity jurisdiction.[1] Unlike the antitrust area, which will be discussed below, there is no federal statute relating to products liability, so if a federal court is to take jurisdiction over such a case, it must be because the litigants happen to be from different states.

As indicated, the number of products liability actions filed in federal court has been growing rapidly in recent years. In fact, cases in federal court on the basis of diversity jurisdiction (i.e., contract *and* tort cases) now constitute about 25 percent of the total federal district court caseload and, according to critics, occupy a disproportionate amount of federal judicial resources. These critics of diversity jurisdiction, which include among them U.S. Supreme Court Chief Justice Warren Burger, argue that diversity should be abolished to help ease crowded court dockets. Legislation in this regard has in recent years twice passed the U.S. House of Representatives but failed in the Senate.

Those who would abolish or at least cut back on diversity jurisdiction argue that, whatever its original purpose, there is in modern times no rational distinction, say, between a defendant in a personal injury/products liability case who happens to be an out-of-state company and one who is an in-state company. In the former case, the parties would have the choice of either a state or a federal forum. In the latter case, because diversity would be lacking, they would be confined to a state court.

Supporters of diversity jurisdiction, including many lawyers and judges, argue that it is still necessary to provide an objective forum in which to air disputes between residents of different states. The problem of clogged federal dockets, they say, can be solved by increasing the number of judges and cutting back in certain areas of federal question jurisdiction.

---

[1] For general discussion of this topic, see Section in Part I entitled "Diversity Jurisdiction."

PART III

LITIGATION IN FEDERAL COURT:
AN ANTITRUST EXAMPLE

This part will view federal court litigation through the perspective of an antitrust case. In Part II, using a products liability example, we focused on the terms and procedures of the various stages of the litigation process. We gave special attention to, among other topics, the class action lawsuit and the latent disease area of products liability litigation.

Here, we will go over similar ground, though focusing on different aspects of a case that is working its way through federal court. We will, for instance, take a closer look at the pretrial process and the actual pleadings filed in a federal court action. As in the previous example, the focus here will be on the civil side of federal litigation, though it should be mentioned that federal antitrust law allows criminal as well as civil actions.

Overview

The first document filed in a civil suit in federal court is the complaint. The complaint gives the general outline of the plaintiff's allegations and names the parties against whom the allegations are made. The supporting facts and issues of law are brought out later in the proceedings. The clerk of the court, once the complaint has been filed, issues a summons, which notifies the defendant that a claim has been made against him and that he must respond or will lose by default. In the federal courts, service is generally made by a U.S. Marshal.

Once a complaint has been made against a party — who becomes the defendant in the action — he has, under the Federal Rules of Civil Procedure, 20 days to file an answer. The answer is the document in which the defendant denies (or admits) the allegations that the plaintiff has raised in the complaint. (See Appendix III for a sample federal court complaint and answer.)

With the filing of the defendant's answer to the plaintiff's complaint, the pretrial phase of the litigation begins in earnest. The pretrial phase consists mainly of the "discovery" process. Discovery, as indicated in the products liability example above, refers to the process through which both sides gather the information necessary to support their respective positions. It may consist of depositions (statements made under oath); interrogatories, or written questions to the parties; and the production of documents. In an antitrust case, discovery may involve months, or even years, of preparation, depending on the complexity of the issues involved.

The objective of the wide-ranging discovery allowed under the Federal Rules of Civil Procedure is to narrow the issues and thereby encourage out-of-court settlements. This avoids the expense of a trial and also serves to ease crowded court dockets. But there are critics of the system who argue that, whatever the theory of discovery, in actual practice it is often being abused, for example, to intentionally string out litigation in an effort to avoid a hearing on the merits of the case and to force the other party to "give in." More on this in the next section.

Problem of Delaying Tactics

While on the subject of discovery, we should mention a major criticism directed at attorneys and federal and state courts alike — that of litigation delaying tactics.

Lawsuits in some instances can drag on for years, during which time legal fees escalate and the resources of the courts are severly strained. This is particularly true in some of the more complex areas of litigation such as antitrust. The median time between the filing of a civil action in federal district court and disposition of the case, whether by decision, settlement, or otherwise (over 90 percent are, in fact, settled prior to trial), is eight months. The median time for antitrust cases, however, is 19 months. It is not unusual for antitrust cases to be in litigation for years, both those between private parties and those filed by the government. The Justice Department's suit against AT&T, for example, ran on for over seven years before a settlement was reached in January 1982.[1] The department's suit against IBM, which charged the company with monopolizing the market for general-purpose digital computers, was 13 years old and in its *seventh year* of trial before a settlement was reached. Both of these cases had been legal battles of epic proportions, involving thousands of technical documents, scores of experts, and lawyers' fees totaling in the millions of dollars.

Some commentators have described the current situation in regard to court delay as outrageous, and efforts are underway to improve it. Prodding has come from as high as the Chief Justice of the U.S. Supreme Court, Warren E. Burger, who in his 1980 end-of-the-year statement warned that "in an era of escalating legal fees and of mounting caseloads, steps to reduce the length of litigation are imperative." The Federal Rules of Civil Procedure has been amended in recent years to give judges greater authority to speed the discovery process. For example, depositions by phone (i.e., "teleconferencing) is now allowed but has thus far gained only limited acceptance. Also, in 1980, Congress passed the Antitrust Procedures Improvement Act which permits the federal courts to assess costs and expenses against the attorney who "multiplies the proceedings...unreasonably and vexatiously." But in order for steps such as these to be effective, judges themselves must show greater willingness to exercise tight, managerial control over their caseloads than many have shown in the past.

A number of state judicial systems, too, are taking steps to prevent costly delays and otherwise speed the litigation process. New York State, however, where a good percentage of the nation's commercial cases are heard, remains one of the worst offenders in this regard.

In discussing certain abuses, however, the worthy objectives of the discovery process should not be lost sight of. Through discovery, parties to litigation lay many of the strengths and weaknesses of their case on the table, early in the proceedings. This encourages settlements, and if a settlement cannot be worked out, promotes a faster and fairer trial.

---

[1]Both the AT&T and IBM settlements were announced by the Justice Department on January 8, 1982. In the AT&T case, the company agreed to divest its 23 local telephone companies but was allowed to retain its long-distance division and its operating subsidiaries, Western Electric and Bell Laboratories. The Justice Department said its suit against IBM was "without merit" and was being terminated.

The Pretrial Conference

When the plaintiff and defendant feel they have gathered adequate material, the presiding judge will hold a pretrial conference. The purpose of the conference is, now that both sides have a good feel for the strength of their respective positions, to simplify the issues and to encourage the parties to settle the case prior to going to trial. Most cases, as indicated, are in fact settled at this stage of the litigation process.

If counsel for each side believes his case is a strong one, he is likely to resist settlement unless the terms offered are favorable. It is typical here for either counsel, or both, to make a motion for summary judgment. This motion asks the court to declare that there is no genuine issue of material fact involved and that the moving party is entitled to judgment in his favor as a matter of law. If this motion is denied, the case is likely to go to trial. Prior to trial, the court would probably require counsel for both parties to file pretrial narrative statements in which the legal issues to be presented at trial and the facts supporting them are discussed in some detail. For sample pretrial narrative statements, see Appendix IV.

The trial, assuming it occurs, would be heard by a jury, or by the judge acting alone. In federal district court a civil jury is composed of six members. The parties, however, may stipulate less than six. Also, unless otherwise stipulated, the verdict of the jury must be unanimous. In a jury trial, questions of law are decided by the court; questions of fact by the jury. Because of the complex issues involved in many antitrust cases, it is not common for counsel to agree that the case be tried without a jury.

Antitrust cases typically involve difficult questions relating to market structure, including the definition of relevant product and geographic markets and the level of market concentration. Still, notwithstanding their protracted nature and complexity, many antitrust cases continue to be tried before juries. Some have argued against jury trials in civil actions of a highly complex nature. They say that such litigation is of a complexity beyond the ability of the average juror to understand and decide rationally and, accordingly, the Seventh Amendment right to trial by jury should be denied or at least severely limited. In a recent holding, a federal appeals court denied plaintiff a right to trial by jury in a civil case involving alleged attempts to monopolize in the sale of electronic products.[1] The court said that in this particular situation, because of the complexity of the issues involved, the constitutional guarantee of due process must take precedence over the constitutional right to trial by jury.

During the trial, each side presents its evidence and argues its respective positions. At the close of arguments, the judge (unless he is trying the case himself) instructs the jury. This involves the judge informing the jury of the principles of law to which they must apply the facts that have been presented in evidence. The verdict of the jury follows. There are two types of verdicts common in federal court practice. One is the general verdict in which the jury renders a decision on the causes of action (i.e., allegations) presented. The other is the

---

[1]*In Re Japanese Electronic Products Antitrust Litigation,* 631 F.2d 1069 (Third Circuit Court of Appeals, 1980).

special verdict, where the judge gives the jury specific factual questions. The jury returns answers to those questions only. The judge then applies the law to those facts as found by the jury.

If the jury cannot reach a verdict, a mistrial is declared and the case, if the plaintiff continues to pursue it, must be tried again. In such circumstances, it would not be uncommon for the parties to reach a settlement rather than go through the expense of a new trial. When the court (i.e., judge) tries the case, the judge must present in writing his findings of fact and conclusions of law. Once the judgment is handed down (judgments are the official announcement of the results of lawsuits), the losing party has 30 days in which to file an appeal. In the federal court system, an appeal from a district court decision is to the U.S. Circuit Court of Appeals that serves that particular district. (See Figure 1, p. 4.)

In a civil action, the plaintiff, in order to prevail, must prove his case by a "preponderance of the evidence." While there is no precise definition of this evidentiary rule, it means that the jury (or judge, if the case is being tried without a jury) must find the existence of the facts in issue more probable than not. The standard of proof in a criminal prosecution is "proof beyond a reasonable doubt," which is more stringent than the civil standard.

Major Antitrust Statutes

There were 1,496 civil antitrust actions filed in federal courts, nationwide in fiscal 1980, an increase of 16.5 percent over 1979. (See Figure 2, p. 11.) Also, there were 39 criminal antitrust cases filed by the Justice Department in fiscal 1980. This is more than any year since 1959 when there were 42 such filings.

Some may consider antitrust to be a rather esoteric area of the law, of concern mainly to "big business." This may have been true decades ago, but it is no longer the case. Litigation under federal antitrust laws has expanded to the extent that businesses of all sizes and types may find themselves involved, as plaintiffs or defendants, or both. Also, a number of states have enacted antitrust/unfair trade laws patterned on the federal statutes. It is advisable, therefore, for businesses, both large and small, that want to avoid problems in this regard to have some knowledge of the antitrust laws and the various activities that may run counter to them.

It is also important for the individual citizen to have some knowledge of federal antitrust law and antitrust litigation. The manner in which antitrust law is enforced can have a nationwide impact on consumer prices and on merger practices. Also, antitrust topics often receive close attention in the press. Prominent among recent antitrust litigation are allegations of anti-competitive practices involving: franchise arrangements of all types, professional fees (including those set by lawyers, engineers, and real estate brokers), exclusion of certain parties from participation in trade associations, price-fixing of auto parts, just to name a few. (A listing of recent antitrust actions is given in Appendix II).

According to Justice Department records, the number of business executives and corporations indicted as a result of Government antitrust prosecutions has increased significantly in the last few years, and the likelihood that individual defendants will receive jail sentences and substantial fines had gone up considerably. The new head of the Justice Department's Antitrust Division, William F.

Baxter, has said the division will continue to scrutinize such activities as price-fixing agreements and bid rigging activity and ask for stiff sentences when appropriate. Maximum penalties available to the Government for a criminal conviction include a fine of $1 million for a corporation, and a fine of $100,000 and three year's imprisonment for an individual.

It is important to note that Government actions against alleged antitrust offenders have a double impact. Not only does the party accused face penalties assessed by the Government, but also he must contend with the numerous treble-damage, private lawsuits that are almost certain to follow, based on the Government's action. Treble-damage means that, should the plaintiff in such a lawsuit prevail at trial, the damages assessed to compensate him for any monetary losses suffered would be automatically trebled by the court. The Sherman Antitrust Act is one of the few federal statutes that allows for treble-damages. This consideration, in practice, encourages many defendants to settle rather than go to trial and risk an adverse decision. Around 90 percent of civil antitrust actions are, in fact, settled prior to trial. The plaintiff, for his part, is often encouraged by the possibility of a treble-damage verdict in his favor to include an antitrust allegation in his complaint even though his major claim may be grounded in some other cause of action, typically breach of contract.

An example of the chain reaction that a government antitrust action can set off is the Cuisinart Food Processor litigation. Early in 1980, the Justice Department persuaded a Hartford, Conn., grand jury to indict Cuisinart for fixing the price of the its popular line of food processors and threatening its distributors if they discounted the product. In December 1980, Cuisinart pleaded no contest and was fined $250,000, the largest fine ever imposed for vertical (i.e., supplier-distributor) price-fixing. This amount, however, could be a drop in the bucket compared to the millions of dollars in damages being claimed against the company in over 20 private civil actions filed subsequent to the Government's suit. Several of these private suits are asking certification as class actions, the class to consist of all purchasers of Cuisinart food processors nationwide.

There are four major federal antitrust statutes: the Sherman Act, the Clayton Act, the Robinson-Patman Act, and the Federal Trade Commission Act. All seek to encourage competition within the nation's economy. The Sherman Act forbids conspiracies in restraint of trade and/or attempts to monopolize. Conspiracies in restraint of trade involve some sort of agreement among competing firms, such as an agreement to fix prices; attempts to monopolize involve unilateral conduct. An example of the latter is the Justice Department's recently-settled action against AT&T, which accused the giant company of attempting to monopolize the communications industry. The settlement calls for AT&T to divest itself of its 23 local telephone companies but be allowed to retain its long-distance division and its operating subsidiaries, Western Electric and Bell Laboratories.

The Clayton Act declares illegal certain tying agreements, i.e., the sale of one product on condition that another be purchased. An example of a tying arrangement that may be subject to challenge under the Clayton Act would be a requirement by a manufacturer of, say, cosmetic products that a dealer distribute its entire line of products or none at all. The Clayton Act also prohibits mergers that tend to substantially lessen competition.

The Robinson-Patman Act prohibits sale of a product at different prices to similarly situated buyers. Enacted in 1936, in the midst of the depression, the Robinson-Patman Act was aimed principally at chain grocery stores that were able to secure favored pricing treatment from suppliers by virtue of their large-volume purchases. The independent grocery stores were thus placed at a competitive disadvantage. The Robinson-Patman Act has had a controversial existence. Its detractors argue that it results, among other things, in higher prices to the consumer. There have been numerous attempts in recent years to amend the Act, but thus far none have been successful. In a recent suit involving Robinson-Patman, a federal jury in Brooklyn, N.Y., found Iowa Beef Processors Inc., the nation's largest beef packer, guilty of offering preferential treatment to one supermarket chain over another, with the result that the latter was driven out of business.

The Federal Trade Commission Act declares unlawful "unfair methods of competition." This is broad authority that covers both antitrust and other areas of unfair trade activities, such as deceptive advertising. Unlike the Sherman, Clayton, and Robinson-Patman Acts, which are enforced in the federal district courts, the FTC Act is enforced at the administrative level, by the Federal Trade Commission. There are no private rights under the FTC Act.

Both the Justice Department and the Federal Trade Commission have overlapping authority in federal antitrust enforcement but attempt to coordinate their activities before undertaking an investigation in this area.

Lawsuits Under the Sherman Act

The great majority of suits filed under the federal antitrust statutes involve private actions alleging violations of Section 1 of the Sherman Act, namely, conspiracies in restraint of trade. The principal restraints of trade which have been found by the courts to be prohibited by Section 1 include: conspiracies affecting prices; agreements to exchange information; agreements to divide markets; and boycotts and other exclusionary practices.

A conspiracy to fix prices may include any combination or agreement that results in prices being raised, stabilized, or depressed. The last situation is often referred to as predatory pricing. Price-fixing also may include the use of fee schedules and value guides promulgated by professional or trade associations. These offenses are often judged by the courts to be "per se" illegal; that is, once the existence of such practices has been shown, the court will consider no evidence of reasonableness or justification in their regard. They are, in other words, presumptively illegal. This legal rule is analogous to the "strict liability" theory discussed in the products liability example above.

In contrast to per se violations, other types of alleged violations of the Sherman Act are generally judged on a "rule of reason" basis. This means that these restraints of trade (examples below) are not per se illegal; that in spite of competitive restraints, such practices may be validated if there are good business reasons for their existence and if the anticompetitive aspects are minimal.

A recent decision of the U.S. Supreme Court has expanded the per se illegality rule to include conspiracies to fix terms of credit to customers. The case involved five beer wholesalers who allegedly banded together to eliminate credit to retailers. A unanimous Court said that an agreement to fix credit terms was no different than an agreement to fix prices and the same per se illegality applied.[1]

Other practices that may unlawfully affect prices, either directly or indirectly, typically involve bid rigging, agreements to control production, and agreements to standardize production. The first two are generally held to be per se illegal; the last is evaluated on a rule of reason basis.

The exchange of price and statistical information among competitors (as is often carried out through trade and professional associations) may or may not be subject to attack under the Sherman Act, depending on the factual situation —i.e., such practices are subject to rule of reason analysis. The systematic exchange of price information has generally been held unlawful absent strong justification. On the other hand, statistical reports on average cost to all member companies without identifying the parties to specific transactions have for the most been upheld by the courts.

Agreements to divide markets or allocate customers may also constitute Sherman Act violations. Horizontal agreements (i.e., agreements among competitors) to divide markets or allocate customers are per se unlawful. An example of an unlawful horizontal agreement would be an exclusive distribution agreement between competitors which restricts one competitor from competing in the market. Vertical (i.e., supplier-distributor) agreements, on the other hand, are subject to the rule of reason analysis.

An example of such a "rule of reason" vertical restraint might involve a manufacturer limiting the distributor to a certain geographical area in which the manufacturer's product may be sold. But a vertical restraint involving a supplier's refusal to deal with a distributor who resold its products at a discount has been held per se illegal. Agreements, however, between a supplier and distributor to exclude a competing distributor are generally subject to rule of reason analysis.

The above examples involve conspiracies (i.e., multifirm conduct) in violation of Sec. 1 of the Sherman Act. A suit involving anticompetitive conduct by a single firm would be filed under Sec. 2, which prohibits monopolization and attempts to monopolize. A rule of thumb holds that in order to be liable under a Sec. 2 monopolization suit, a firm must control around 90% of the relevant market. More typical of Sec. 2 litigation are suits involving attempts to monopolize. An example of the latter would be an action by a cancelled distributor against the supplier. If, however, the distributor alleges that the supplier conspired with others in this regard, then the action would probably be filed under Sec. 1 of the Sherman Act as well as Sec. 2.

Mention was made of the Clayton Act section that prohibits mergers that tend to substantially lessen competition. The Justice Department under the Reagan Administration has indicated that it will not be as active in challenging corporate mergers as have previous administrations. William F. Baxter, the Assistant Attorney General for Antitrust, has said that the Government should stay out of the way of most vertical mergers, in which one company buys another that is

---

[1] *Catalano v. Target Sales*, #79-1101, May 27, 1980.

involved in its supply, production, or marketing chain. A shoe manufacturer's acquisition of a chain of shoe stores, for instance, would presumably fall into this "let-alone" category.

Baxter believes that vertical mergers rarely foster price-fixing or reduce competition. He feels similarly about "conglomerate" mergers, in which a corporation buys a concern in an entirely different line of business. But Baxter does favor, as have previous Antitrust Division chiefs, tough Government action in cases of horizontal mergers, in which one corporation acquires a direct competitor, and strict prosecution for price-fixing and other collusive action among competitors.

A Hypothetical Antitrust Case

For our sample antitrust action, we will set up a hypothetical case and follow it through the various stages of litigation. The issues involved in the typical antitrust case are, as indicated, quite complex, and the example given here is, of necessity, highly simplified.[1] The example does, however, illustrate a basic type of antitrust lawsuit that is becoming increasingly common: disputes involving supplier-distributor and franchiser-franchisee agreements.

The plaintiff in our hypothetical case is Brooks Office Supply Co. (Brooks), located in the imaginary county seat of Jefferson County, in the State of Franklin. Brooks is a distributor of office products supplied by defendant Abacus International, a large multinational conglomerate corporation. Our antitrust case begins when plaintiff Brooks files a suit in federal court against defendant Abacus, alleging a number of antitrust violations in regard to their dealer-supplier relationship. The plaintiff's complaint and the defendant's answer are given in Appendix III.

Brooks alleges a number of unlawful actions on the part of Abacus, including the following: (1) that Abacus was involved in a conspiracy in violation of the Sherman Act to fix the retail prices of Abacus' products and to require Brooks to sell at the prices so determined; (2) that Brooks was prevented from selling Abacus' products outside a specific designated territory; (3) that Abacus conspired to prevent independent dealers, such as Brooks, from selling products that competed with Abacus' product line; and (4) that there was an illegal tie-in arrangement in regard to Abacus' requirement that in order to be given the right to distribute one of the company's major products, Brooks had to agree to distribute other products supplied by Abacus as well. Plaintiff Brooks further argues that its refusal to adhere to defendant's set prices and territorial limitations was the proximate cause of its being terminated as an Abacus dealer, and that extensive monetary damages in lost profits have thereby resulted.

Defendant Abacus in its answer gives a general denial to the plaintiff's allegations. After the discovery process, which will be discussed below, both plaintiff and defendant will more definitively present their respective positions in pretrial narrative statements. (See Appendix IV.) In its statement, Abacus responds to the allegations as follows: (1) In answer to the price-fixing allega-

---

[1]This example is based on the "Trial of an Antitrust Case", *Antitrust Law Journal* (American Bar Assoc.), Vol. 46, Issue 1 (1977).

tion, Abacus contends that it merely "suggested" certain prices to be charged for its products and that dealers were not required to adhere to the prices so suggested; (2) concerning plaintiff's claim of unlawful territorial restrictions, defendant explains that such restrictions were necessary in order to place reasonable limits on the obligation of dealers to service the Abacus products they sold; (3) defendant Abacus answers plaintiff Brook's claim that dealers were prevented from selling competing products by a general denial of the facts so alleged; and finally, (4) in regard to the illegal tie-in allegation, defendant responds that this was basically a marketing strategy, intended to give Abacus dealers necessary experience in selling a full line of related products.

The price-fixing allegation of plaintiff Brooks is potentially the most serious, the most difficult to defend against. The legal significance of this allegation is that it is generally viewed as a per se offense. The territorial restriction and tie-in claims of plaintiff, on the other hand, will likely be judged on a "rule of reason" basis. (For discussion of per se and rule of reason offenses, see above pages 42 and 43).

The Discovery Process

Once defendant Abacus answers plaintiff Brook's complaint, the discovery process begins in earnest. The discovery process, as indicated, refers to the gathering of information by plaintiff and defendant in order to develop the evidence necessary to support their respective positions. In antitrust litigation it is not unusual for discovery to go on for months, if not years, and involve considerable legal costs.

Through their attorneys, both parties to the litigation would want to depose (i.e., take depositions of) the other's chief executive officers. The CEO for Brooks, for example, would be asked in a deposition if any representative of Abacus ever told him he would lose his dealership if he sold Abacus products at less than the suggested list price. This issue, the crux of the price-fixing allegation, would be further developed at trial should the litigation proceed to that stage.

In addition, one or other of the parties would want to bring into evidence certain documents, such as the retail distributor franchise agreement between Brooks and Abacus and correspondence between the companies related to this agreement. Defendant Abacus would want to produce evidence that it was aware of the antitrust laws and took special steps to ensure that its employees complied with them. In this regard, it would offer into evidence a memorandum sent to employees concerning compliance with the antitrust laws. (See Appendix V.)

Plaintiff Brooks must not only prove his allegations against defendant but must prove also that he was damaged by defendant's actions in the amount so claimed. In this regard, plaintiff would produce an expert's report thoroughly estimating these damages, which, of course, would be tripled should the case go to trial and the judgment come down in plaintiff's favor. This report would include estimates of profits lost by Brooks both as a result of Abacus' (alleged) refusal to allow it to carry competing lines and as a result of restricting it to a certain territory of operation. Concerning the price-fixing allegation, plaintiff would claim that the price set by defendant was unreasonably high and caused plaintiff to lose sales that it otherwise would have had at a lower, more reasonable price level. Should the case go to trial, both sides would have expert witnesses further testify in this regard.

At the close of discovery, or after the process has gone on for some time, both sides would generally be in a good position to size up the relative strength of their cases. This is the very purpose of the discovery process: to narrow the points of contention and to encourage settlements, thus avoiding the time and expense of a trial. Most cases are, in fact, settled at this stage of the litigation.

But while discovery, which is governed by the Federal Rules of Civil Procedure, does often serve to encourage settlements and avoid unnecessary litigation, many argue that the process has gotten out of hand; that discovery has become a "trial by combat," in which the litigant most able to afford the necessary expense will engage in endless rounds of discovery requests. In response to this criticism, some tightening in the rules governing the civil discovery has taken place; but according to some critics — including Supreme Court Justice Lewis F. Powell — the changes did not go nearly far enough.

The Trial

If the parties cannot reach a settlement, the next step is to proceed to trial. Either party could request a trial by jury. Otherwise, the case will be heard by the presiding judge. In a civil proceeding such as this, the plaintiff, in order to prevail, must prove his case by a preponderance of the evidence.

A trial would be based on, and involve a further development of, the material gathered by the parties during the discovery process; there are few surprises in antitrust litigation. After closing arguments in a case tried before a jury, the presiding judge would instruct the jury in the law to be applied to the facts as presented.

Even with a jury, the judge remains firmly in command of the litigation proceedings. While a party may have the right to a jury trial, this does not necessarily include the right to have a jury render a verdict in the lawsuit. That right exists only if the judge believes there is something for the jury to decide. If, for instance, at the conclusion of the trial the judge feels that the plaintiff had not made an even minimal case in support of its allegations, he could, on defendant's motion, grant a directed verdict for the defendant. When the credibility of witnesses figures heavily in the trial, however, it is almost impossible to obtain a directed verdict, as this is a matter for the jury's consideration. Even after the verdict, the judge can grant the judgment he feels the case calls for, notwithstanding the jury's verdict, or he may order a new trial.

An example of the use of the directed verdict is seen in a recent antitrust suit that Memorex Co. brought against IBM. In that suit, the jurors voted 9-2 in Memorex's favor before declaring themselves deadlocked. The normal procedure in such circumstances would be for the court to declare a mistrial and order a new trial. But the judge in this case, after interviewing each juror, went further: he declared the jurors ignorant of the basic facts of the case and awarded IBM a directed verdict. This action, though quite unusual in federal court litigation, points up not only the judge's strong authority but also the growing concern among many involved in antitrust litigation that such cases often go beyond the average juror's ability to comprehend.

Most antitrust cases, perhaps as a reflection of their complexity, are tried by the court itself, with no jury. The actual trial in such a case is much the same as with a jury, though there are no jury selection problems, no instructions, and no verdict as such. In a non-jury case, the presiding judge must give a fairly detailed statement of his findings of fact and conclusions of law. This statement may be oral or written, though usually the latter. Any appeals from the jury's verdict or judge's decision must be made within 30 days of judgment to the appropriate U.S. circuit court of appeals. Appeal from a circuit court decision is, of course, to the U.S. Supreme Court.

CONCLUSION

GUIDE TO THE FEDERAL COURTS has pointed up the dramatic expansion in federal court litigation during the past decade. This increase is explained in part by the rise of litigation in several established areas of the law and in part by the enactment of new laws. Congress, in fact, passed over 70 statutes during the past decade that granted federal jurisdiction over matters where none before existed.

The overlapping of federal court and state court litigation was discussed. The antitrust/unfair trade example represented a case in federal court on the basis of "federal question" jurisdiction, while the products liability case was in federal court on the basis of "diversity" jurisdiction.

Attention was given to the recent increase in the number of authorized federal judgeships and the growing importance of the federal magistrate as a judge's assistant.

Also, we looked at a number of other matters relating to the federal litigation process, including: the burden being put on federal courts, and state courts as well, by latent disease actions; the pros and cons of the class action lawsuit; million-dollar jury verdicts; and the problems associated with federal court "discovery" and court delay.

GUIDE TO THE FEDERAL COURTS is intended as a reading and reference source on the federal judiciary system. The appendices include a Glossary of Terms and other handy material for those wishing additional information.

APPENDIX I

FEDERAL COURT GLOSSARY OF TERMS

ACTION:	Case - cause - suit - controversy. A question or dispute contested before a court of justice.
ACQUITTAL:	Equivalent to legal certification of innocence.
AFFIDAVIT:	A written statement of facts confirmed by the oath of the party making it, before a notary or other officer having authority to administer oaths.
AFFIRMED:	In the practice of appellate courts, to affirm a judgment, decree or order, is to declare that it is valid and right and must stand as rendered in the lower court.
ALLEGATION:	A claim or statement of what a party intends to prove; the facts as one party claims they are.
ALLEGE:	To claim or declare that something is so (Whether it is actually so will have to be proved later.)
AMENDMENT:	The correction of an error in any process, pleading, or proceeding at law.
ANSWER:	The formal written statement made by a defendant setting forth the grounds for his defense.
APPEAL:	A review by a higher court of the judgment or decision of a lower court.
APPELLANT:	The party who takes the appeal to the higher court.
APPELLEE:	The party against whom the appeal is taken.
ARRAIGNMENT:	A proceeding in which the criminal defendant is called into court, the indictment is read to him and he is called on to plead.

Source: Administrative Office of the U.S. Courts

ARREST:

Taking physical custody of a person, by legal authority, for the purpose of holding him to answer a criminal charge.

BAIL:

To obtain the release of a person from legal custody by giving security that he will appear on the day and time appointed.

BILL OF PARTICULARS:

A statement of the details of the charge made against the defendant.

BOND:

A certificate or evidence of a debt; a written promise to pay a certain amount of money if certain conditions are not met.

BOND FOR COSTS:

A bond given by a party to secure the eventual payment of the costs of the suit.

BRIEF:

A written summary of the case, including a statement of the facts, a statement of the questions of law involved and the arguments and authorities upon which the party relies. It serves as the basis for an argument in the appellate court and is filed for the information of the Court.

CAPIAS:

A writ requiring the marshal to take a defendant into custody.

CHALLENGE:

An objection. As we use it here, it is an objection to a juror summoned to try the case.
CHALLENGE FOR CAUSE: A challenge to a juror for which some cause or reason is alleged.
PEREMPTORY CHALLENGE: A challenge to a juror without alleging any cause or reason; a limited number of peremptory challenges is allowed each side in any case.

CHARGE TO THE JURY:

The judge's instruction to the jury concerning the law which it is to apply to the facts of the case.

CITE:

(1) To command the presence of a person; to notify a person of legal proceedings against him and require his appearance thereto.
(2) To read or refer to legal authorities in an argument to a court. For example, to cite a case is to refer to that case in an attempt to persuade the Court to be guided by the decision reached in that case.

CIVIL ACTION:

Every law suit other than a criminal action; an adversary proceeding for the enforcement or protection of a right or the redress or prevention of a wrong.

CLERK OF COURT:

An officer of a court of justice who has charge of the clerical part of its business, who keeps its records and seal, issues process, enters judgments and orders, gives certified copies from the record, etc.

COMPLAINANT:

The party who complains or sues; one who applies to the Court for legal redress, also called the PLAINTIFF.

COMPLAINT:

A formal written statement in which the plaintiff gives the facts as he believes them to be and demands the relief to which he believes he is entitled. This is the beginning of the suit.

CONVICTION:

A judgment of guilt against a criminal defendant.

COSTS:

An amount of money awarded to the successful party (and recoverable from the losing party) for certain of his expenses in prosecuting or defending the suit.

CROSS-EXAMINATION:

After a witness has given evidence, the attorney for the opposing party examines or questions him about his evidence, to test its truth or to add to it or for some other purpose.

CROSS-CLAIM:

A claim by one party against a co-party (one defendant claiming against another defendant, or one plaintiff against another plaintiff) arising out of the occurrence in the original complaint.

COUNTER-CLAIM:

A claim which the defendant makes against the plaintiff.

COURT OF APPEALS: An intermediate court, inferior to the United States Supreme Court, but higher than the United States District Court. Its function is to review and pass upon the correctness or error of the decisions of the district courts. The United States is divided into eleven judicial circuits. In each there is established a court of appeals known as the United States Court of Appeals for the circuit.

DAMAGES: A compensation in money, which may be recovered in the courts by a person who has suffered loss or injury through the unlawful act or negligence of another.

DIVERSITY OF CITIZENSHIP: A phrase used with reference to jurisdiction. It means that all the persons on one side of the case are citizens of states different from all the persons of the other side.

DEPOSITION: Generally, a statement made orally by a person under oath before an officer of the court, but not in open court, taken down in writing by the officer or at his direction. The attorney for the opposing party is notified to attend and he may cross-examine the deposed party. The deposition may be used later in the trial of the case, or it may be taken only to obtain discovery.

DISCOVERY: The disclosure by one party of the facts, titles, documents, etc., exclusively within his knowledge, to the opposing party who needs this information to properly prosecute or defend the case.

DISTRICT COURTS: Courts of the United States, each having territorial jurisdiction over a district which may include a whole state or part of it. The district court sees and hears the testimony of the witnesses, receives the documents and other exhibits, etc., and makes its determination. It is distinguished from an appeals court, which reviews a case from the record of a completed case.

DOCKET: A book in which brief entries of all court proceedings are recorded.

DEFENDANT: The person defending or denying; the party against whom relief or recovery is sought in a civil action or suit; the party who is accused in a criminal suit.

DOCUMENT: Generally refers to writings, pictures, maps, etc., sometimes denotes official papers such as deeds, agreements, title papers, receipts and other written instruments used to prove a fact.

ENTRY OF JUDGMENT: Recording the judgment; the clerk's putting into the docket book a statement of the final judgment.

EVIDENCE: Any kind of proof, legally presented at trial, through witnesses, records, documents, etc., for the purpose of persuading the court or jury of the correctness of the contentions of the parties.

EXAMINATION: An investigation or search; the examination of a witness consists of the series of questions put to him by a party to the action or his attorney, for the purpose of bringing before the court and jury in legal form the knowledge which the witness has of the facts and matters in dispute, or of probing and sifting his evidence previously given.

EXECUTION: The completion, fulfillment or perfecting of anything. Execution of judgment is a writ (order) to the marshal or sheriff requiring him to carry out the judgment of the Court.

FEDERAL QUESTION: Refers to jurisdiction given to the federal courts over cases involving the interpretation and application of the United States Constitution and Acts of Congress.

FILE: To put into the files or records of the court; to file a paper is to place it in the official custody of the clerk. The clerk is to endorse upon the paper the date it is received, and retain it in his office, subject to inspection by whomsoever it may concern.

HABEAS CORPUS: A writ, ordering that a person in custody be brought before the Court; usually used to bring a prisoner before the Court to determine the legality of his imprisonment. May also be used to bring a person in custody before the Court to give testimony, or to be prosecuted, etc.

HEARING: A relatively formal proceeding similar to a trial, with one or more issues to be determined.

IMPEACH: To impeach a witness is to question the truthfulness or correctness of his testimony.

IN FORMA PAUPERIS: In the manner of a pauper. Describes permission given to a poor person to sue without payment of costs.

IN REM: An action in rem is one taken directly against property, and has for its object the disposition of property, without reference to who might be the owner of the property.

INDICTMENT: The formal charging of the defendant with a particular crime by a grand jury.

INFORMATION: The formal accusation charging the defendant with a particular crime, but brought by the U.S. Attorney, rather than by the grand jury.

INJUNCTION: An order of the Court forbidding the performance of some specific act. It is issued for the purpose of preventing irreparable damage. It may be temporary or permanent.

INTERVENTION: A proceeding in a suit by which a third party is permitted to make himself a party to a suit pending between other parties. He may join the plaintiff seeking what is sought in the complaint, or with the defendant, resisting the claims of the plaintiff, or demanding something adverse to both of them.

INTERROGATORIES: Written questions asked by one party and served on an opposing party, who must answer them in writing under oath.

ISSUE:

(1) The disputed point or question to which the parties to a case have narrowed their disagreement; a single material point which is affirmed by one side and denied by the other. When plaintiff and defendant have arrived at some point which one affirms and the other denies, they are said to be "at issue". When defendant has filed an answer denying all or part of the allegations of the complaint, we say "issue has been joined" and the case is ready to be set for trial.
(2) To send out officially. Example: to issue an order.

JUDGMENT:

The official and authentic decision of a Court upon the respective rights and claims of the parties to a suit.
DEFAULT JUDGMENT: A judgment rendered because of the defendant's failure to answer or appear.
SUMMARY JUDGMENT: Judgment given on the basis of pleadings, affidavits and exhibits presented without any need for going to trial. It is used when there is no dispute as to the facts of the case and one party is entitled to judgment as a matter of law.

DECLARATORY JUDGMENT: A judgment which declares the rights of the parties without ordering anything to be done.
CONSENT JUDGMENT: The provisions and terms of the judgment are agreed on by the parties and submitted to the Court for its sanction and approval.

JURISDICTION:

The power or authority of the Court to hear and decide a case.

JURY:

A certain number of people selected according to law and sworn to inquire into certain matters of fact and declare the truth upon matters laid before them.
PETIT JURY: a group of people, impaneled and sworn in a district court to try to determine any question or issue of fact, in any civil or criminal action according to law and the evidence given them in the court.
GRAND JURY: so called because it is made up of a larger number of persons. The grand jury hears the government's evidence against a person who is accused of a crime and determines whether it is sufficient to justify bringing that person to trial.

ISSUE:

(1) The disputed point or question to which the parties to a case have narrowed their disagreement; a single material point which is affirmed by one side and denied by the other. When plaintiff and defendant have arrived at some point which one affirms and the other denies, they are said to be "at issue". When defendant has filed an answer denying all or part of the allegations of the complaint, we say "issue has been joined" and the case is ready to be set for trial.
(2) To send out officially. Example: to issue an order.

JUDGMENT:

The official and authentic decision of a Court upon the respective rights and claims of the parties to a suit.
DEFAULT JUDGMENT: A judgment rendered because of the defendant's failure to answer or appear.
SUMMARY JUDGMENT: Judgment given on the basis of pleadings, affidavits and exhibits presented without any need for going to trial. It is used when there is no dispute as to the facts of the case and one party is entitled to judgment as a matter of law.

DECLARATORY JUDGMENT: A judgment which declares the rights of the parties without ordering anything to be done.
CONSENT JUDGMENT: The provisions and terms of the judgment are agreed on by the parties and submitted to the Court for its sanction and approval.

JURISDICTION:

The power or authority of the Court to hear and decide a case.

JURY:

A certain number of people selected according to law and sworn to inquire into certain matters of fact and declare the truth upon matters laid before them.
PETIT JURY: a group of people, impaneled and sworn in a district court to try to determine any question or issue of fact, in any civil or criminal action according to law and the evidence given them in the court.
GRAND JURY: so called because it is made up of a larger number of persons. The grand jury hears the government's evidence against a person who is accused of a crime and determines whether it is sufficient to justify bringing that person to trial.

OPINION:

A formal statement of the reasons upon which the judgment is based.

PARTIES:

The persons who take part in any act or performance. Here it means the plaintiff and defendant - the persons who are actively concerned with the prosecution or defense of the suit.

PLAINTIFF (OR COMPLAINANT):

The one who brings the suit, asking for enforcement of a right or recovery of relief from a wrong.

PLEA:

In a criminal proceeding it is the defendant's declaration in open court, either that he is guilty or that he is not guilty - the defendant's answer to the charges made against him in the indictment or information.

PLEADING:

The name given to any of the formal written statements presented by the parties in a civil case -- complaint, answer, counter-claim, cross-claim. All such statements together are termed "the pleadings".

PRELIMINARY EXAMINATION (OR PRELIMINARY HEARING):

A hearing given to a person accused of a crime, by a magistrate or judge, to determine whether there is evidence to warrant holding the person. It is a course of procedure whereby a possible abuse of power may be prevented.

PRE-TRIAL CONFERENCE:

An informal conference between the attorneys for both sides, with the judge as moderator, to clarify and narrow the issues and to attempt to work out a settlement in cases where this would be practical.

PROBATION:

A clemency or mercy shown by the Court by which convicted defendants are released on suspended sentences generally under the supervision of a probation officer as long as they observe certain conditions.

PROCEEDING:

The conducting of a judicial business before the Court or judicial officer; any step or act taken in a lawsuit from the beginning to the execution of the judgment.

PROCESS:

As used here it signifies the summons or any other writ which may be issued during the progress of the case.

PROCEDURE:

The machinery for carrying on the suit; the rules, customs, etc., which regulate the manner of conducting the suit.

QUASH:

To annul or make void.

RECORD:

A written memorial of all the acts and proceedings in an action or suit.

REMAND:

To send back. The act of the appellate court in sending a case back to the district court for some further action there.

RETURN:

The act of the marshal or other officer delivering back to the Court the writ or notice, or other paper which he was required to serve, with a brief account of his doings under it - the time and manner of service or the reason why he was not able to serve it.

REVERSAL:

The act of an appellate court annulling a judgment of a lower court because of some error.

SERVICE:

The delivery of a writ, notice, injunction, etc., by an authorized person to a person who is thereby officially notified of some action or proceeding in which he is concerned.

SERVICE OF PROCESS:

The service of writs, summonses, rules, etc., to the party to whom they ought to be delivered.

SUBPOENA:

A command to a witness to appear and give testimony.

SUBPOENA DUCES TECUM:

A command to a witness who has in his possession or control some document or paper that is pertinent to the issues of a pending case, to produce it at the trial or hearing.

SUMMONS:
A writ directed to the marshal requiring him to notify the person named that an action has been commenced against him in the court, and that he is required to appear, on a day named, and answer the complaint in such action.

SUPPRESS:
To put a stop to a thing actually existing; a motion to suppress evidence or a confession which does not deny the existence of the evidence or confession, but asks the Court not to allow them to be used in the case.

TEMPORARY RESTRAINING ORDER:
Prohibits a person from doing something which is likely to cause irreparable harm. Differs from an injunction in that it may be granted immediately, without notice to the opposing party and without a hearing of any sort; it is intended to last only a few days - until a hearing can be held.

TESTIMONY:
Oral evidence given by a witness under oath; as distinguished from evidence derived from writings.

TRANSCRIPT:
Literally, a copy of any kind. As we commonly use the term, it refers to the typewritten transcription of the shorthand notes made by the court reporter of the proceedings in court.

VENUE:
The geographical location in which a case is tried.

VERDICT:
The formal decision or finding made by the jury upon the matters or questions submitted to them upon the trial.

VOIR DIRE:
The preliminary examination which the Court makes of one summoned as a juror to determine his competency, interest, etc., to serve on a particular case.

WRIT:
A formal written command, issuing from the Court, requiring the performance of a specific act.

APPENDIX II

RECENTLY-FILED CASES

This appendix includes selected, recently-filed cases brought in federal courts around the country. These cases were extracted from the weekly publication, *Federal Filings Alert* (WANT Publishing Co., Washington, D.C.), which reports comprehensively on new federal court filings in a number of areas of the law, including antitrust/unfair trade and products liability, among others.

Learning of cases soon after they are filed enables one to follow a particular case of interest through the various stages of the litigation process. Most documents filed in a case are placed on the public record and are often a valuable source of information, particularly in the law and business areas.

The average time between the filing of a case in federal court and its disposition, by decision, settlement or otherwise, is eight months. However, in the more complex areas of litigation, such as antitrust and products liability, cases can drag on for years.

The cases included below — first for antitrust/unfair trade and then for products liability — are listed alphabetically by State. The first case listed below, for example, was filed in the U.S. District Court for Arizona, in the Phoenix office. The second case listed was filed in the U.S. District Court for the Northern District of California (California is divided into four districts), in the San Francisco office. Following the case summary is the date the case was filed.

ANTITRUST/UNFAIR TRADE

Ariz(Phoenix): *Harkins Amusement Enterprises Inc. v. General Cinema Corp. et al.* Plaintiff alleges that defendant exhibitor of motion pictures conspired with major distributors to fix price and terms re showing of motion pictures in metropolitan Phoenix, Ariz. 9/29/80.

NCal(San Francisco): *Western Builders Inc. v. Alside Inc. et al.* In suit filed as class action, plaintiff alleges conspiracy to fix price of exterior siding and related building products. Other defendants include Aluminum Co. of America and Bethlehem Steel Corp. 12/9/80.

NCal(San Francisco): *Collection Computers Inc. v. Sperry Rand Corp.* Plaintiff contends that defendant refused to supply it with its computers for resale unless plaintiff agreed not to carry competing lines and to sell defendant's products at set prices. 8/11/80.

NCal(San Francisco): *FTC v. H.N. Singer Inc. d-b-a Hot Box Products, et al.* In its first enforcement action under the 1979 franchise rule, the FTC alleges fraud in regard to the sale of worthless frozen-pizza distributorships. 7/30/80.

ECal(Sacramento): *California v. Pendleton Woolen Mills Inc.* In suit filed as class action, California claims that Pendleton conspired to fix price of certain apparel products and blankets. 7/22/80.

DC(District of Columbia): *U.S. v. Am. Consulting Eng. Council.* Challenge to Code of Ethics of defendant organization on basis that it restricts competition in market for engineering consulting services. 8/15/80.

NGa(Atlanta): *GMC Fun Center Inc. v. Champion Home Builders Co. et al.* Plaintiff alleges that defendant sold recreational vehicles in plaintiff's exclusive territory in violation of manufacturer-dealer agreement. 7/14/80.

NIll(Chicago): *Warner Management Consultants Inc. v. Data General Corp. et al.* Allegation of restraint of trade re tying purchase of equipment to that of other leasing and financial services. 9/4/80.

SIll(Rock Island): *City of Flora(Ill.) et al v. Central Illinois Public Service Co.* Plaintiff cities claim violation of Robinson-Patman Act re dual prices higher than that charged retail customers. 7/10/80.

SInd(Evansville): *Blairex Laboratories Inc. v. Bausch & Lomb Inc.* Allegation of restraint of trade and false advertising re products for heat disinfection of soft contact lenses. 10/6/80.

Mass(Boston): *Stop & Shop Companies Inc. v. Roblin Industries Inc. et al.* Plaintiff supermarkets allege, in suit filed as class action, that defendants conspired to fix price of shopping carts. 10/1/80.

Mass(Boston): *Goldstein et al v. Exxon Co. et al.* Plaintiff dealer contends antitrust violations re conspiracy to fix resale price of gasoline sold by Exxon dealers and lease of gasoline service stations on condition that dealers refrain from purchasing products from competitors of Exxon. 7/2/80.

EMich(Detroit): *Am. Production Welding Corp. v. Zurich Am. Insurance Co. of Illinois et al.* Plaintiff alleges conspiracy to fix the price of worker's compensation insurance and to deny competing underwriters and insurers an opportunity to compete for same. 6/20/80.

EMich(Chicago): *Glen Eden Hospital v. Blue Cross & Blue Shield of Michigan Inc.* Plaintiff alleges a conspiracy to fix a noncompetitive reimbursement mechanism to participating hospitals unrelated to quality of patient care and to boycott hospitals that do not participate in such reimbursement mechanism. 6/10/80.

EMo(St. Louis): *High Technology Inc. v. Apple Computer Inc.* Plaintiff distributor alleges antitrust violations re territorial restrictions and refusal of defendant to allow it to carry competing line of computer products. 6/23/80.

EMo(St. Louis): *Schaulat et al v. Burger Chef Sys. Inc.* Plaintiffs, independent franchises of defendant, allege that defendant has attempted to drive them out of business through such means as refusing to grant franchises in profitable areas. 6/27/70.

NJ(Newark): *Independent Cash Register Dealers Assoc. v. Sharp Electronics Corp.* Plaintiff contends that defendant set sales quotas for its electronic cash registers in violation of distribution agreement and otherwise attempted to monopolize market for same. 2/27/81.

SNY(New York City): *U.S. v. New York County Lawyers' Assoc.* The Justice Dept. charges defendant with conspiring to restrict trust and estate services which corporate fiduciaries may provide to the public in competition with lawyers. 10/20/80.

NOhio(Cleveland): *U.S. v. First National Supermarkets Inc. et al.* The Justice Dept. charges defendants with conspiracy to fix prices for retail sale of grocery and meat products. 10/10/80.

NOhio(Cleveland): *Jameson et al v. Sommer's Mobile Home Sales et al.* Plaintiffs allege restraint of trade re trying sale of mobile homes to lease of space in mobile home park. 7/24/80.

EPa(Philadelphia): *Arthur Treacher's Fish & Chips Inc. v. Arthur Treacher's Franchise Assoc. et al.* Action against class of Arthur Treacher's franchisees who have allegedly failed to comply with royalty agreements and have attempted to control prices and supplies for Arthur Treacher's restaurants. 3/19/81.

NTex(Dallas): *Lacy-Logan Inv. et al v. Frito-Lay Inc. et al.* Plaintiffs allege a conspiracy to fix the price of vegetable oil. 11/12/81.

Wyo(Cheyene): *U.S. v. Laramie County Liquor Dealers Assoc.* Allegation of price fixing re defendant's "suggested retail price list" for beer, wine, and liquor. 8/11/80.

PRODUCTS LIABILITY

WArk(Fayetteville): *King v. Lederle Laboratories et al.* Plaintiff claim she developed poliomyelitis as result of contact with her child after he was immunized by live poliovirus vaccine sold under trade name ORIMUNE. 1/19/81.

Ariz(Tucson): *Williams v. Snap-On Tools Corp. et al.* Hand injury caused by allegedly defective wrench and mechanic's tool set. 8/1/80.

NCal(San Francisco): *Thompson et al v. Procter & Gamble Co. et al.* In suit filed as class action, plaintiffs allege that defendant failed to warn of dangers associated with use of Rely tampons. 9/23/80.

ECal(Sacramento): *Moura v. Smithkline Corp.* Plaintiff claims he suffered injury to his liver and kidney through ingestion of drug Selacryn, which had been prescribed for treatment of hypertension. 1/6/81.

Colo(Denver): *Alley v. Best Mobile Homes et al.* Plaintiff alleges toxic levels of urea-formaldehyde insulation were used in mobile home. Other defendants are Gypsum Co. and Weyerhaeuser Co. 7/25/80.

DC(District of Columbia): *Carroll v. Division Seven Inc. et al.* Plaintiff, an insulation installer, claims he was injured in explosion of adhesive material known as Bituthene PBA-3000, manufactured by W.R. Grace Co. 3/11/81.

NGa(Atlanta): *Morrison v. Eli Lilly & Co. et al.* Plaintiff alleges that she developed cancer as result of her mother having injested drug DES during pregnancy for prevention of miscarriage. 6/10/80.

SIll(Alton): *Hayes v. Bayer Co.* Products liability action re alleged failure to provide adequate warnings re use of Bayer Timed-Release Aspirin. 1/29/81.

Kans(Kansas City): *Troutman v. Syntex Laboratories Inc.* Plaintiff minor alleges he was injured through consumption of Neo-Mull-Soy baby food. 11/12/80.

Kans(Kansas City): *McDonnell v. Sunbeam Corp. et al.* Plaintiff claims burn injuries were suffered through use of defective heating pad. 3/25/81.

EMich(Detroit): *Murray v. Upjohn Co.* Injuries allegedly caused by use of antibiotic drug "Lincocin." 6/2/80.

EMich(Detroit): *Waelde v. Merck, Sharp & Dohme.* Allegation that death from leukemia was induced by Clinoril (sulindac), a non-steroidal anti-inflammatory prescription drug. 3/18/81.

WMich(Marquette): *Caffey v. Motorola Inc.* Plaintiff claims that malfunction of electrical system caused television set to catch fire. 2/19/81.

Minn(Minneapolis): *Simon v. G.D. Searle & Co.* Plaintiff alleges she suffered hysterectomy as a result use of intrauterine device known as "CU-7." 3/6/80.

NJ(Newark): *Lear v. Hoffman-LaRoche Inc. et al.* Plaintiff claims that defendant failed to provide warnings re dependence and addiction allegedly associated with uyse of Valium at therapeutic levels. 3/6/81.

NH(Concord): *Paquette v. General Electric Co.* Plaintiff claims he suffered burns as a result of defective deep fat fryer. 8/7/80.

NM(Albuquerque): *Howl v. Deseret Co.* Allegedly defective catheter manufactured by defendant caused breakage and lodging in plaintiff's heart valve. 2/9/81.

ENY(Brooklyn): *Donato v. The Toro Co.* Defendant allegedly created unreasonable risk by failing to design "Home Pro" lawn mower to prevent inadvertent contact by operator with rotating blades. 9/29/80.

NOhio(Cleveland): *Hughes v. Combustion Engineering Inc. et al.* Plaintiff alleges he contracted asbestosis as a direct result of exposure to asbestos insulation products. Other defendants include Johns-Manville Corp. 5/23/80.

NOkla(Bartlesville): *Waltman v. Bic Pen Corp.* Allegation of injury re explosion of defective cigarette lighter. 7/2/80.

NOkla(Tulsa): *Foster v. Textron Inc.* Plaintiff was injured by allegedly defective chainsaw (Homelite Model XL). 9/19/80.

EPa(Philadelphia): *Kesselman v. International Sport & Safety Equipment Ltd.* Allegation of design defect in motorcycle helmet and helmet strap. 10/1/80.

NTex(Dallas): *Marcum v. Montgomery Wards & Co. et al.* Plaintiff alleges defendant Scott & Fetzer Co. failed to provide adequate guard grill for Montgomery Ward Airless (paint) Sprayer. 1/16/81.

APPENDIX III

UNITED STATES DISTRICT COURT FOR THE SOUTHERN DISTRICT OF FRANKLIN

. . . .

BROOKS OFFICE SUPPLY COMPANY, INC., a corporation,)	) Civil Action No. 74 Civ. 1553
Plaintiff,)	)
v.)	) COMPLAINT
ABACUS, INC., a corporation,)	)
Defendant.)	)

. . . .

Plaintiff, for its Complaint avers:

For a First Claim for Relief:

1. This action arises under the antitrust laws of the United States, more specifically sections 1 and 2 of the Act of Congress of July 2, 1890, commonly known as the Sherman Act, 15 U.S.C. §§ 1 and 2, and section 3 of the Act of Congress of October 15, 1914, commonly known as the Clayton Act, 15 U.S.C. § 14. The jurisidiction of this Court is invoked under and is conferred by sections 4 and 12 of the Clayton Act, 15 U.S.C. §§ 15 and 22, and 28 U.S.C. § 1337.

2. Plaintiff, Brooks Office Supply Company, Inc., is now and has at all times material hereto been a corporation organized and existing under the laws of the state of Franklin, with its principal place of business in River City, Jefferson County, Franklin.

3. Plaintiff was engaged at all times material hereto in the business of retail distribution of office supplies and equipment.

4. Defendant, Abacus, Inc., (hereinafter Abacus) is a corporation organized and existing under the laws of the State of Delaware, with its principal

Source: *Antitrust Law Journal* (American Bar Assoc.), Vol. 46, Issue 1 (1977)

place of business in San Francisco, California, and is now and at all times material hereto was doing business in and found in the State of Franklin.

5. Defendant Abacus is and at times material hereto was engaged in the importation, development, manufacture and marketing of office and commercial equipment including but not limited to the following products (the "Products"): typewriters, adding machines, electronic calculators, addressing machines, electronic memory typewriters, electronic cash registers, dictating and transcribing equipment, and dry photocopiers.

6. The acts alleged in this complaint to have been done by Defendant were authorized, ordered and done by the officers, agents, employees or representatives of Defendant, all actively engaged in the management, direction or control of its affairs.

7. Plaintiff has been a retail distributor of various of Defendant's Products since before 1959, and on July 1, 1959 was designated exclusive retail dealer of certain Products in specified counties in the State of Franklin (the "Territory") pursuant to the terms of a "Retail Distributor Franchise Agreement" (the "Franchise Agreement"). A copy of such Franchise Agreement is attached hereto as Exhibit A, and is incorporated herein by reference. The terms and conditions of such Franchise Agreement were modified and amended in writing from time to time as reflected in revisions of the Franchise Agreement, dated January 1, 1962, January 1, 1964, August 1, 1968, and January 2, 1969 ("Franchise Agreements"), copies of which are attached hereto as Exhibits B, C, D and E, respectively and are incorporated herein by reference.

8. Defendant occupies a dominant position in the sale of certain Products in the Territory.

9. Prior to its appointment as exclusive retail distributor of Defendant's Products, Plaintiff was a retail dealer for various Products marketed by persons other than Defendant, but at Defendant's insistence relinquished such dealerships under threat of losing the Abacus dealership. Defendant has from time to time threatened Plaintiff with loss of the Abacus dealership if Plaintiff undertook to distribute Products marketed by persons other than Defendant.

10. By means of the actions described in paragraph 9 hereof, Defendant has imposed upon Plaintiff and coerced Plaintiff into acquiescing in an understanding and agreement that Plaintiff would not sell Products marketed by any persons other than Defendant.

11. On numerous occasions Plaintiff was approached by companies desiring to distribute their products through Plaintiff. Plaintiff refused to do

so because of the understanding and agreement referred to in paragraph 10 hereof.

12. As a result of Defendant's imposition of the understanding and agreement that Plaintiff was not permitted to become a dealer for other companies, competitors of Defendant were foreclosed from selling through Plaintiff, who was uniquely successful in selling the Products in the Territory, and Plaintiff was foreclosed from distributing the Products of such companies.

13. The effect of such understanding and agreement was to restrain interstate trade or commerce and substantially to lessen competition or tend to create a monopoly in the sale of the Products distributed by Plaintiff.

14. Plaintiff was damaged in its business or property by the imposition of the above-mentioned understanding and agreement.

For a Second Claim for Relief:

15. Plaintiff repeats and reavers the averments of paragraphs 1-14 hereof.

16. In November, 1973, Plaintiff became the exclusive retail dealer for office copiers manufactured and marketed by Crampton & Holland, Inc., which are in competition with office copiers manufactured by Defendant.

17. After Plaintiff had accepted the Crampton & Holland dealership, Defendant on numerous occasions threatened to terminate Plaintiff's Abacus dealership unless it ceased selling Crampton & Holland copiers. Plaintiff has refused to relinquish its Crampton & Holland dealership.

18. By letter dated August 21, 1974 (attached herto as Exhibit F), Defendant purported to terminate Plaintiff's dealership pursuant to paragraph 13 of the Franchise Agreement, effective September 30, 1974.

19. The cause or a substantial contributing cause of said termination, and of the damage which said termination has caused to Plaintiff, was the refusal of Plaintiff to abide by the agreement or understanding not to distribute Products marketed by any person other than or competing with Defendant, which agreement or understanding violates Section 1 of the Sherman Act and Section 3 of the Clayton Act.

20. Plaintiff expended substantial amounts of money, labor, and effort to establish and maintain a distribution system for Abacus Products, to establish and maintain good will toward Abacus and its Products and to promote the continued sale of same.

21. The termination of Plaintiff's Abacus dealership injured Plaintiff in its business or property.

For a Third Claim for Relief:

22. Plaintiff repeats and reavers the averments of paragraphs 1-8, 18 and 20 hereof.

23. Immediately prior to the purported termination of Plaintiff's dealership Abacus Products were distributed through various authorized dealers, including Farr Business Supply Co., Hemlock Falls, Franklin ("Farr").

24. Defendant has since approximately 1959 combined, conspired and agreed with its authorized dealers to restrain interstate trade and commerce in Abacus Products within the Territory and within the territories of the other dealers. More particularly, Defendant and its dealers have combined, conspired and agreed to place territorial restrictions upon the dealers' sales of Products purchased from Defendant.

25. In formulating and effectuating the aforesaid combination, conspiracy and agreement Defendant and its dealers did those things which they combined, conspired and agreed to do, including, among other things, the following:

(a) Prior to January 1, 1964, the Franchise Agreements provided as follows:

"6. The DEALER shall not sell, offer for sale, solicit sales of PRODUCTS nor appoint agents or representatives for such purposes outside the Territory set forth in Schedule B. The MANUFACTURER shall not appoint any other dealer in said Territory for the PRODUCTS listed in Schedule A. . . ."

(b) The Franchise Agreements dated January 1, 1964, August 1, 1968 and January 2, 1969 provided as follows:

"6. The DEALER is authorized to sell, offer for sale, solicit sales of PRODUCTS and appoint agents or representatives for such purposes within the Territory set forth in Schedule B. The MANUFACTURER shall not appoint any other dealer in said Territory for the PRODUCTS listed in Schedule A. . . ."

(c) Defendant has repeatedly informed Plaintiff that Defendant would consider sales of Products by a dealer outside the dealer's designated territory as evidence that the dealer was not using his best efforts to sell Defendant's Products within the dealer's territory as required by Paragraph 8 of the Franchise Agreement, and hence would be the basis for terminating the dealership.

(d) Upon information and belief, Abacus and its other dealers have entered into dealership contracts with similar provisions since approximately 1959.

(e) Defendant was able to enforce compliance with its territorial restrictions as to some of its Products because as to such Products its standard practice was to ship directly to the ultimate customer rather than to the dealer; thereby it was aware of and could control any sales which dealers attempted to make outside their territories. As to the other Products, Defendant was able to use its warranty card system (whereby upon delivery of the Product, in order to validate the warranty, the customer sent to Defendant a card which included the name of the dealer) to maintain records of sales outside of authorized territories.

(f) Plaintiff from time to time made sales to customers from outside its designated Territory. The profit upon sales made to such customers, in whole or in part, was allocated by Defendant to the dealer located in the same territory as the cusomer.

26. Defendant's policy of enforcing an understanding or agreement restricting the territories of its dealers was a violation of sections 1 and 2 of the Sherman Act and has resulted in loss of sales by Plaintiff to potential customers outside the Territory and loss of profits to Plaintiff.

27. The termination of Plaintiff's Abacus dealership injured Plaintiff in its business or property.

For a Fourth Claim for Relief:

28. Plaintiff repeats and reavers the averments of paragraphs 1-8, 18, 20 and 23 hereof.

29. Defendant has since at least 1959 combined, conspired and agreed with its dealers to restrain interstate trade and commerce in the Abacus Products within the Territory and the territories of the other dealers, in violation of Section 1 of the Sherman Act. More particularly, Defendant and its dealers have combined, conspired and agreed to fix retail prices of the Abacus Products.

30. In formulating and effectuating the aforesaid combination, conspiracy and agreement, Defendant and its dealers did those things which they combined, conspired and agreed to do, including, among other things, the following:

(a) The Franchise Agreements entered into between Plaintiff and Defendant prior to August 1, 1968 provided:

"2. The DEALER shall purchase PRODUCTS at the then current discounts from list as issued by the MANUFACTURER from time to time and shall resell PRODUCTS in the Territory described in Schedule B on the reverse hereof at the established list prices as released by the MANUFACTURER from time to time, said prices being exclusive of any forwarding and freight charges from MANUFACTURER'S warehouse, costs of installation, finance charges or sales or excise taxes applicable to sales of PRODUCTS, which said charges or taxes shall be added to said prices. DEALER shall upon sale of PRODUCTS to others than ultimate users obtain the agreement of the purchasers not to resell PRODUCTS except at the established list prices as determined above."

(b) On July 18, 1967, Defendant notified Plaintiff that the Franklin Fair Trade Act had been repealed as of July 1, 1967 and that fair trade prices could no longer be enforced, but that list prices for Abacus Products would remain unchanged.

(c) The Franchise Agreements entered into between Plaintiff and Defendant on August 1, 1968 provided:

"2. The DEALER shall purchase PRODUCTS at the then current discounts from list as issued by the MANUFACTURER from time to time, said prices being exclusive of any forwarding and freight charges from MANUFACTURER'S warehouse, costs of installation, finance charges or sales or excise taxes applicable to sales of PRODUCTS, which said charges or taxes shall be added to said prices."

(d) Defendant has imposed such provisions upon Plaintiff as part of Defendant's standard dealership contracts.

(e) Upon information and belief, Defendant and its other dealers have entered into dealership contracts with similar provisions since approximately 1959.

(f) Since approximately 1959, Defendant, Plaintiff, and, upon information and belief, Defendant's other dealers agreed and understood that the dealer's prices to their customers would be fixed by Defendant.

(g) Defendant's practice has been to permit discounts from its list prices only when approved in advance by Defendant, which in such cases agreed to absorb some of the discount from list which the dealer was permitted to give to the customer.

(h) Defendant refused to permit discounts from list, or to absorb any of the discount from list, except where the dealers submitted to Defendant a copy of the customer's order which evidenced the discount granted by the dealer.

31. Defendant has been firm and resolute in enforcing its policy that its dealers sell at prices set by Defendant and has coerced its dealers to adhere to that policy by means, inter alia, of

(a) the practice described in paragraphs 30(a) through 30(h), and

(b) the threat imposed by its power to terminate the dealerships upon thirty days' notice.

32. Because of the price-fixing scheme described above, Plaintiff has in many instances been unable to meet competition in its pricing and has lost sales in a substantial amount.

33. Notwithstanding Defendant's refusal to permit Plaintiff to sell below list, Plaintiff has from time to time sold Abacus Products below list, beginning in 1972, to which sales Defendant has repeatedly objected. Since Plaintiff began selling Products below list Defendant has repeatedly sought Plaintiff's acquiescence in Defendant's price-fixing scheme.

34. The cause or a substantial contributing cause of Defendant's termination of Plaintiff's Abacus dealership was Plaintiff's unwillingness to adhere to the prices established by Defendant.

35. The termination of Plaintiff's dealership injured Plaintiff in its business or property.

For a Fifth Claim for Relief:

36. Plaintiff repeats and reavers the averments of paragraphs 1-8, 18, 20 and 23 hereof.

37. Defendant has since approximately 1959 combined, conspired and agreed with its dealers to restrain interstate trade and commerce within the Territory and the territories of the other dealers, in violation of Section 1 of the Sherman Act and Section 3 of the Clayton Act. More particularly, Defendant has imposed upon its dealers an understanding and agreement that if they act as dealers for any of the Abacus Products, some of which are unique and protected by patents and know-how from being duplicated by Abacus' competitors, they will be required to act as dealers for the full line of Abacus Products.

38. In formulating and effectuating the aforesaid combination, conspiracy and agreement, Defendant and its dealers did those things which they combined, conspired and agreed to do, including, among other things, the following:

(a) The Franchise Agreements entered into between Plaintiff and Defendant provide:

"1. MANUFACTURER hereby appoints DEALER to be an exclusive dealer of its Products listed in Schedule A. . . .

"3. ... The MANUFACTURER at any time and from time to time by written notice to the DEALER may eliminate or add PRODUCTS to Schedule A. ...

"4. In order to round out the line the MANUFACTURER will from time to time appoint the DEALER to sell other products under the brand-name ABACUS or other brandnames on a non-exclusive basis and, these will be listed on Schedule C on the reverse hereof. The MANUFAC-TURER may eliminate or add PRODUCTS to schedule C from time to time."

(b) Defendant imposed such provisions upon Plaintiff as part of Defendant's standard dealership contracts.

(c) Upon information and belief, Defendant and its other dealers have entered into dealership contracts with similar provisions since approximately 1959.

(d) In 1970, Defendant became the exclusive United States distributor for a desk model dry photocopier ("Copier 1000"), sold in the United States under the Abacus trademark. Pursuant to the understanding and agreement described in paragraph 37, Defendant in November of 1970 required Plaintiff to undertake to sell Copier 1000. Plaintiff was required to expend substantial sums in preparation for selling Copier 1000 and to hire a new sales/serviceman for that purpose.

39. Plaintiff at no time desired to sell Copier 1000.

40. In October of 1973, Defendant set a date of January 1, 1974 for reexamining Plaintiff's efforts and results with respect to the Copier 1000.

41. The disagreements over selling the Copier 1000 coupled with Defendant's refusal to permit Plaintiff to handle less than the full line of Products offered by Defendant was the cause or a substantial contributing cause of Defendant's purported termination of Plaintiff's dealership for all Abacus Products.

42. The termination of Plaintiff's dealership injured Plaintiff in its business or property.

For a Sixth Claim for Relief:

43. Plaintiff repeats and reavers the averments of paragraphs 1-8, 18, 20, 23 and 24.

44. In formulating and effectuating the aforesaid combination, conspiracy and agreement, Defendant and its dealers did those things which they com-

bined, conspired and agreed to do, including, among other things, the following:

(a) The Franchise Agreement of January 1, 1969 provided as follows:

"6. The DEALER is authorized to sell, offer for sale, solicit sales of PRODUCTS and appoint agents or representatives for such purposes within the Territory set forth in Schedule B. The DEALER agrees to maintain its place of business at 13 E. College St., River City, Franklin, and shall not establish any other place of business dealing in the Products unless DEALER obtains written approval from MANFACTURER. The MANU-FACTURER shall not appoint any other dealer in the Territory assigned to DEALER for the PRODUCTS listed in Schedule A. . . . "

(b) Defendant imposed such provisions upon Plaintiff as part of Defendant's standard dealership contracts.

(c) Upon information and belief, Defendant and its other dealers have entered into dealership contracts with similar provisions since approximately 1969.

(d) In August, 1971, Plaintiff opened a branch store at Hochdorf, Jefferson County, Franklin, from which it sold primarily office supplies but in which it demonstrated some Abacus Products. Orders for the purchase of Products were accepted only at 13 E. College St., River City, Franklin.

(e) Defendant repeatedly asserted that Plaintiff was selling Abacus Products from the Hochdorf branch in Breach of the provisions set forth in paragraph 44(a).

45. Defendant entered into an agreement or understanding with Farr that if Plaintiff did not cease demonstrating Abacus Products at the Hochdorf branch, Defendant would terminate Plaintiff's Abacus distributorship.

46. Plaintiff's demonstration of Abacus Products at Plaintiff's Hochdorf branch was the cause or a substantial contributing cause of Defendant's purported termination of Plaintiff's distributorship.

47. The termination of Plaintiff's dealership injured Plaintiff in its business or property.

WHEREFORE, Plaintiff prays:

A. That the Court adjudge and decree that Defendant has monopolized and attempted and conspired with others to monopolize the sale of Products in violation of Section 2 of the Sherman Act and has engaged in an unlawful combination, conspiracy and agreement in restraint of aforesaid interstate trade and commerce in violation of Section 1 of the Sherman Act and Section 3 of the Clayton Act.

B. That the Court adjudge that Defendant's violation of sections 1 and 2 of the Sherman Act and Section 3 of the Clayton Act injured Plaintiff in its business or property in the amount of at least one million dollars.

C. That Plaintiff recover threefold the damages determined to have been sustained by them, together with reasonable counsel fees and the costs and disbursements of this action, and that judgment be entered against Defendant for the amount determined.

Jury Trial Demanded

November 15, 1974

Clarence DeLyver

Thomas A. Atkins

Stande & DeLyver
2130 Grand Avenue
Franklin City, Franklin
Attorneys for Plaintiff

IN THE UNITED STATES DISTRICT COURT
FOR THE SOUTHERN DISTRICT OF
FRANKLIN

. . . .

BROOKS OFFICE SUPPLY CO.,   )
)
                Plaintiff,   )   Civil Action No. 74 Civ. 1553
)
v.   )
)
ABACUS, INC.,   )
)
                Defendant.   )

. . . .

A N S W E R

Defendant, Abacus, Inc., by its attorney, DeLahy, Lenger & Waite, hereby answers Plaintiff's Complaint as follows:

1. Denies each and every averment of paragraph 1, except that this action allegedly arises under the antitrust laws of the United States.

2. Admits the averments of paragraphs 2, 3, 4, 7, 18, 23 and 40.

3. Denies that Defendant Abacus, Inc. is now or was at any time subsequent to 1957 engaged in the manufacture of any of the products listed in paragraph 5; admits the remaining averments of paragraph 5.

4. Denies each and every averment of paragraph 6, except as to acts admitted herein as having been done by Defendant.

5. Denies each and every averment of paragraphs 8, 10, 12, 13, 14; the first sentence of paragraph 17; paragraphs 19, 21, 24, 26, 27, 29, 31, 32, 34, 35, 37, 39, 41 and 42, 45, 46 and 47.

6. Denies each and every averment of paragraph 9 except states that it lacks knowledge or information sufficient to form a belief as to the truth of the averment that prior to its appointment as exclusive retail distributor of Defendant's Products, Plaintiff was a retail dealer for various Products marketed by persons other than Defendant.

7. Denies the existence of any understanding or agreement referred to in paragraph 11 and states that it lacks knowledge or information sufficient to form a belief as to the truth of the remaining averments of paragraph 11.

8. Repeats and reavers its answers to the paragraphs referred to in paragraphs 15, 22, 28, 36 and 43.

9. States that it lacks knowledge or information sufficient to form a belief as to the truth of the averments of paragraph 16, the second sentence of paragraph 17 and paragraph 20.

10. With respect to paragraph 25, denies formulating and effectuating any combination, conspiracy or agreement in restraint of trade; admits that the Franchise Agreements there referred to contained the language quoted in paragraphs 25(a) and (b); admits that Defendant shipped some Products directly to the ultimate customer and that customers were required to send a warranty card to Defendant to validate the warranty, which card included space for the dealer's name but denies that Defendant required the customer to include the name of the dealer; admits the first sentence of paragraph 25(f) and admits that a portion of the dealer discount on some of such sales was credited to the dealer having primary responsibility for the sale and service of Products in the territory in which the customer was located, to compensate such dealer for its expenditures in promoting the sale of Products within its territory and the warranty and other services that such dealer might be called upon to render; and denies all other averments of paragraph 25, including specifically each and every averment of paragraphs 25(c) and (d).

11. With respect to paragraph 30, denies formulating and effectuating any combination, conspiracy or agreement in restraint of trade; admits that the Franchise Agreements there referred to contained the language quoted in paragraphs 30(a) and (c); admits that on or about July 15, 1967, Defendant notified all its franchised dealers in the State of Franklin, including Plaintiff, that the Franklin Fair Trade Act had been repealed as of July 1, 1967, that Defendant would no longer enforce fair trade prices, and that suggested list prices for Abacus Products (from which dealer discounts were calculated) would remain unchanged; and denies all other averments of paragraph 30, including specifically each and every averment of paragraphs 30(d), (e), (f), (g), and (h).

12. Denies each and every averment of paragraph 33 except admits that Plaintiff has from time to time sold Abacus Products below suggested list price.

13. With respect to paragraph 38, denies formulating and effectuating any combination, conspiracy or agreement in restraint of trade; admits that

the Franchise Agreements there referred to contained the language quoted in paragraph 38(a); admits the averments of paragraph 38(c) and the first sentence of paragraph 38(d); states that it lacks knowledge or information sufficient to form a belief as to the truth of the third sentence of paragraph 38(d); and denies all other averments of paragraph 38, including specifically each and every averment of paragraph 38(b) and the second sentence of paragraph 38(d).

14. With respect to paragraph 44, denies formulating and effectuating any combination, conspiracy or agreement in restraint of trade; admits that the Franchise Agreements there referred to contained the language quoted in paragraph 44(a); admits the averments of paragraphs 44(c) and (e); states that it lacks knowledge or information sufficient to form a belief as to the truth of the averments of paragraph 44(d), except that from time to time Plaintiff demonstrated Abacus Products at Plaintiff's Hockdorf store; and denies all other averments of paragraph 44, including specifically each and every averment of paragraph 44(b).

FOR A FIRST DEFENSE:

14. The complaint fails to state a claim upon which relief can be granted.

FOR A SECOND DEFENSE:

15. Avers that all claims for damages resulting from purchases prior to the period prescribed by Section 4(B) of the Clayton Act are barred and should be dismissed and that all references in the complaint to any transactions prior thereto should be stricken.

WHEREFORE, Defendant Abacus, Inc. demands judgment dismissing the complaint, together with costs and disbursements.

December 18, 1974

DELAHY, LENGER & WAITE

by _____
A Member of the Firm

Attorneys for Defendant
Abacus, Inc.
   3715 Enterprise Tower
   Franklin City, Franklin

APPENDIX IV

UNITED STATES DISTRICT COURT FOR THE SOUTHERN DISTRICT OF FRANKLIN

. . . .

BROOKS OFFICE SUPPLY COM-)		
PANY, INC., a Corporation,)		Civil Action No. 74 Civ. 1553
)		
Plaintiff,)		
)		
v.)		
)		
ABACUS, INC., a Corporation,)		
)		
Defendant.)		

. . . .

PLAINTIFF'S PRETRIAL NARRATIVE STATEMENT

AND NOW, comes Plaintiff,- and for its Pretrial Narrative Statement states as follows:

FACTS

Plaintiff Brooks Office Supply Co., Inc. is a local office equipment and supply dealer located in River City, the county seat of Jefferson County, in the State of Franklin. River City has a population of approximately 42,000. It is the home of Franklin State University. There is no heavy industry located in River City nor in Jefferson County. There are a number of firms engaged in light manufacturing, including, for example, a corrugated box manufacturer, a commercial book bindery, and a small plastics products fabricator. There are also a number of service establishments in River City and the immediately surrounding area, including two engineering consulting firms, a nationally known testing and measurement establishment, two data processing service concerns, a mutual insurance company, a major warehouse and distribution center for a large retail grocery chain, a small beef processing plant, and a number of wholesale and retail establishments which serve the permanent population of River City, the 20,000 students attending Franklin State University, and the families in the contiguous counties to the east, south and west for whom River City is the primary shopping center.

Source: *Antitrust Law Journal* (American Bar Assoc.), Vol. 46, Issue 1 (1977)

Brooks Office Supply Company was founded by the grandfather of Rufus Brooks II as a proprietary stationery shop in 1903. Over the years, with changes in the economy and in technology, Brooks Office Supply Co. changed and expanded to meet the needs of its customers. It began carrying business equipment, primarily typewriters, in 1938. Following World War II a machine maintenance department was added so that Brooks Office Supply Co. could provide repair and servicing of the office equipment which it sold. By that time it stocked duplicating and addressing machines and mechanical adding machines, as well as typewriters. Brooks Office Supply Co. was incorporated as Brooks Office Supply Company, Inc., (hereinafter "Brooks") a Franklin corporation, in 1956.

Rufus Brooks II, the president and principal stockholder, acceded to the presidency of Brooks in 1958. Under his leadership Brooks has undertaken a major expansion program in order better to serve the growing demands of the business, academic and commercial community. Recognizing that the projected increase in the size of the student body of Franklin State University (to accommodate the World War II "baby boom") would in turn stimulate rapid growth in the economy of River City and contiguous areas, Brooks enlarged its office equipment and fixtures department, adding office furniture as well as additional machine lines. Particular attention was devoted to emphasizing quality and reliability of the equipment and furniture which it handled and to eliminate from its lines those brands which did not measure up to its standards of quality.

In 1958 Brooks was appointed as an exclusive dealer for Abacus Corporation (hereinafter "Abacus") as to typewriters, adding machines and cash registers. At that time, Abacus was a closely-held corporation which was owned and managed by the Marshall family. It had originally been called Marshall Business Machines and had been run by the Marshalls for several generations. It had attained a wide reputation in the business community for producing a high quality product which was very reliable and required a minimum of service. Brooks had handled Marshall business machines (and Abacus machines after the change of name) for a number of years prior to the exclusive dealership arrangement.

Under the terms of the agreement with Abacus, Brooks was to be Abacus' exclusive representative in the counties of Jefferson, Madison and Monroe. Brooks was required to use its best efforts to promote the sale of Abacus products within the territory and was flatly prohibited from selling or even soliciting sales of products outside the three counties. Brooks was required to adhere to prices established by Abacus under the Franklin Fair Trade Law in its advertising and sales and was to require those who purchased the products for resale to agree that the products would not be resold except at the list prices established by Abacus. Brooks was further required to maintain a service department and to maintain an inventory of accessories and replacement parts for Abacus. In order to carry out its obligation to give its best efforts to the sale of Abacus equipment, Brooks was required to give up its handling of all competing brands of typewriters and adding machines. (Brooks was not at that time handling cash registers of other makes.)

In 1962 Abacus was taken over by Abacus International (at that time known as Superior Products), a large multinational conglomerate corporation with its headquarters in Tokyo. Immediately after the take-over, Brooks was informed that it could no longer sell Abacus equipment to Franklin State University, although up to that time the University had been Brooks' largest and most reliable customer. Brooks' sales territory was nominally extended by the addition of Jackson County, a predominantly agrarian area with little demand for office equipment.

There followed a series of revisions in the dealership agreement, which Brooks was offered on a take-it-or-leave-it basis. In 1964 the contractual language which had unequivocally prohibited Brooks from selling outside its territory was modified, but company personnel repeatedly made it clear to Brooks that if it in fact sold outside its designated territory, it would be viewed as a failure to comply with the contractual requirement that it use its "best efforts" to sell Abacus equipment within Brooks' assigned area. As a further inhibition upon Brooks' ability to sell to customers located outside the area unilaterally designated by Abacus, the dealership agreements in 1964 and thereafter contained a coercive "pay-over" provision under which the dealer was required to pay half its commission on such sales to the dealer assigned to the territory in which the customer was located.

In 1967, the State of Franklin's Fair Trade Law was repealed. Abacus sent its dealers formal notification that the resale price maintenance provision contained in the dealer contracts was no longer enforceable. Brooks received such a notification, and it will be introduced as an exhibit. The document itself makes clear that dealers were in fact being told that they could *not* cut prices. This understanding was reinforced by Abacus personnel at national sales meetings, in conversations with dealers, and by letters and memoranda.

In 1969, Abacus introduced an entirely new line of electronic office equipment. Most of this equipment was manufactured in Japan. Most of the lines were modifications of equipment which had originally been marketed

In 1971, Brooks opened a branch office in the little town of Hochdorf on the northern edge of Jefferson County. The county immediately to the north is Adams County of which the principal urban area is Hemlock Falls. Brooks opened the Hochdorf branch primarily as an outlet for stationery and other office supplies in order to serve the growing community of commercial establishments and small service organizations which was arising in the corridor between River City and Hemlock Falls. The Hochdorf branch was located in a shopping plaza and catered to a large extent to walk-in customers. However, as a result of the quota system, Brooks was under considerable pressure to increase its sales of Abacus products. Accordingly, Brooks maintained a display of Abacus equipment in its Hochdorf branch and undertook a limited sales effort out of that branch in hopes of increasing its sales of Abacus equipment.

Brooks was not interested in aggressively pursuing sales in Adams County because of the punitive pay-over provisions of the Abacus dealership contract, which required Brooks to pay 50% of its sales commission to the Hemlock Falls franchise dealer on each sale made in Adams County. However, Brooks hoped to increase its sales in Hochdorf itself and the contiguous areas within Jefferson County. Occasionally sales of Abacus equipment were made to customers whose business was located in Adams County, and Brooks duly paid over one half of its sales commission to Farr Business Supply (hereinafter "Farr"), the Hemlock Falls dealer. Nevertheless, such sales invariably resulted in a visit, telephone call or letter from the Abacus district sales representative or regional manager complaining that Brooks was not using its best efforts in its own territory. Discovery in this case has revealed that such communications by Abacus to Brooks were typically preceded by communications in some form between Farr and Abacus personnel. The Abacus representative repeatedly pointed out that Brooks' Abacus franchise was limited by the dealership agreement to River City and that the sales out of the Hochdorf branch were thus in violation of the agreement. Brooks thereupon reluctantly ceased its equipment sales efforts out of its Hochdorf branch, although it continued to maintain a display of Abacus equipment there. Potential buyers were referred to the River City office, and all sales activities, as well as inventory and service facilities, were maintained at the River City office.

Brooks was able to exceed its sales quotas on all Abacus products except the Copier 1000 in 1972. But in order to do so it was compelled to sponsor a year end office equipment sale, where all office equipment was reduced by 10% off the suggested retail price. That event prompted another communication from Abacus personnel that the Brooks branch office in Hochdorf violated the location clause in Brooks' contract. Again, at Farr's initia-

in Europe and Asia, during which the imperfections had been largely eliminated. Consequently, most of the equipment lines represented high quality, reliable products. Brooks' president and its other sales/service personnel recognized the potential which the electronic equipment introduced by Abacus possessed, and Brooks launched a significant sales effort. This effort soon began to bear fruit and in 1970 Brooks' sales of office equipment jumped by more than 20 percent over the preceding year.

Although Brooks was successful overall in marketing Abacus' new lines of electronic equipment, there was one line which was not up to the quality standards of the rest of the equipment. This was the desk photocopier, called "Copier 1000". Unlike the other equipment, this item was an entirely new piece of equipment which had been developed primarily for the American market and which had not undergone substantial use and testing in Europe and Asia before being launched in this country. It quickly became apparent to Brooks' personnel that the Copier 1000 contained many engineering shortcomings and that it was not competitively priced with other photocopying equipment on the market. Brooks' president pointed out to Abacus immediately and frequently that the Copier 1000 was not of the quality that both Abacus and Brooks had been accustomed to marketing. Consequently, Brooks was having little success in distributing it. Brooks was losing money on it and in the longer run losing valuable customer good will because of its poor performance, and hence was not interested in carrying the copier until its quality was substantially improved. However, the dealership agreement included a provision which required dealers to handle all equipment lines designated by Abacus. Thus, Brooks was required to use its best efforts to sell a copier which it believed to be unsatisfactory.

This problem was further compounded by the institution of a system of quotas in 1970. Under this system, each dealer was required to notify Abacus of the volume of sales that it anticipated it could make over the coming year. Abacus then produced a figure based upon its unilateral judgment as to the dealer's sales potential for the coming year. Where Abacus' figure was higher than the dealer's, Abacus' figure prevailed and became the quota. Brooks repeatedly experienced having its proposed quota rejected and a higher quota substituted by Abacus. This was particularly a problem with respect to the Copier 1000 which Brooks believed it could not effectively market. Nevertheless, in every year up until 1973, Abacus increased Brooks' quota on the Copier 1000, even though Brooks had never been able to achieve its quota on that product. Even in 1973, Abacus did not reduce the quota for the copier. The unrealistic 1972 quota was merely carried forward. In 1974, for the first time, Abacus agreed to a decrease in Brooks' overall quota, including its quota for the copier.

tive, Abacus wrote Brooks about Brooks' off list price sales, pointedly reminding Brooks that adequate profit margins had to be maintained to offer effective service functions. Brooks was also told at this time that if Brooks did not stop selling at discount prices and selling outside its territory, Brooks' dealership would be in jeopardy.

Abacus came out with a new copier in 1973. While some of the bugs had been worked out of the new machine, Brooks still experienced extensive customer complaints about the Abacus photocopier. In efforts both to combat the deepening recession and to retain its customers with photocopier needs, Brooks began to carry a photocopier manufactured by one of Abacus' competitors. It also continued to make occasional Abacus sales at less than the prescribed list price.

Brooks' president was quite vocal at the fall 1973 regional sales meeting about Abacus' (1) failure to produce a quality photocopier and (2) failure to become price competitive despite the downtrodden economy, complaints in which other dealers joined. The only response Mr. Brooks elicited, however, was a terse letter from Abacus to the effect that Brooks wasn't trying hard enough. Abacus also informed Brooks that Abacus was reexamining the "relationship" between Brooks and Abacus. The reexamination was to have been completed by January 1, 1974. Brooks continued as an Abacus dealer on that date. Brooks' target quotas for 1974—unchanged from 1973—were unilaterally set by Abacus. Still faced with a declining economy, Brooks made more sales at prices below list. It also took advantage of any sales opportunities arising out of the Hochdorf branch. Whenever a sale at the Hochdorf office turned out to be a sale to a "Farr customer," Brooks duly paid over 50% of the commission to Farr.

In light of its continuously unprofitable experience with Abacus' copier and Abacus' unresponsive attitude toward its dealers' problems in promoting it, Brooks finally decided that it could no longer afford to carry it. Abacus' only response was to argue the supposed benefits of full line marketing; again, however, Abacus questioned the Hochdorf branch.

In midyear 1974, Abacus introduced a new dictation system, to which Brooks was contractually entitled to be the Jefferson County dealer. However, Brooks was *not* supplied with the new product. Rather, Farr, the Hemlock Falls Abacus dealer, became the Jefferson County dealer for the new product. Thereupon Farr opened a River City branch store, as first step toward taking over Brooks' Abacus dealership entirely. Shortly after Brooks again started making Abacus sales off list price, it was notified of its termination as an Abacus dealer, effective October 1, 1974. Farr immediately became the new exclusive dealer of Abacus products for Brooks' former territory. In fact, Farr had been informed by Abacus that it would receive this territory in February of 1974. Farr's entry was attended by extensive local advertising by Abacus.

As a result of the unlawful restrictions placed upon it by Abacus, Brooks experienced in 1974 its first net loss in its entire history. It also ended 1975 in the red. By 1975 Brooks had been able to secure a new office machinery product line, but it was neither as well known nor as extensive as Abacus.

The Complaint. Plaintiff has set forth six claims for relief in its complaint. Claims one and two allege a conspiracy to foreclose independent Abacus dealers, including Brooks, from selling products which competed with Abacus' products. They allege that the initial adherence by Plaintiff injured it in its business and property through lost sales and profits, and that Plaintiff's subsequent refusal to adhere was a proximate cause of its termination, causing Plaintiff further injury in its business and property. The third claim alleges a conspiracy between Abacus and its dealers to foreclose Plaintiff from selling Abacus' products outside of Plaintiff's designated geographical territory or to customers reserved to Defendant. It alleges that Plaintiff's initial adherence injured Plaintiff in its business and property through lost sales and profits, and that Plaintiff's sales outside its geographical territory was a proximate cause of its termination as an Abacus dealer. Claim four alleges a conspiracy between Abacus and its dealers to fix the retail prices of Abacus products. It alleges that Plaintiff's initial adherence injured it in its business and property through lost sales and profits, and that Plaintiff's subsequent refusal to adhere to Abacus list prices was a proximate cause of its termination as an Abacus dealer. Claim five alleges a contract or conspiracy to compel Plaintiff to promote and sell all Abacus products, whether desired by Plaintiff or not. It alleges that Plaintiff specifically did not desire to promote or sell Abacus' Copier 1000 because, *inter alia,* it was a defective and overpriced product; and that Plaintiff's initial acquiescence resulted in its promoting and selling the Copier 1000, which injured Plaintiff in its business and property through exorbitant sales and service costs, lost sales and profits, and substantial loss of Plaintiff's goodwill; and that Plaintiff's subsequent refusal to promote and sell Defendant's copier was a proximate cause of its termination. The sixth and final claim alleges a contract in restraint of trade imposed upon Plaintiff by Abacus under which Plaintiff was prohibited from selling Abacus products at its Hochdorf branch, and a conspiracy between defendant Abacus and Farr to the effect that if Plaintiff failed to cease and desist from promoting Abacus products in Plaintiff's branch store in Hochdorf, Defendant would terminate Plaintiff's Abacus dealership. It alleges that Plaintiff's initial acquiescence in this restriction injured Plaintiff in its business and property and that Plaintiff's subsequent failure to acquiesce was a proximate cause of its termination as an Abacus dealer.

The Damages

A. Pretermination damages resulting from Defendant's refusal to allow Plaintiff to carry competitive products.

Defendant throughout its relationship with Plaintiff enforced a *de facto* foreclosure of Plaintiff's distributing products competitive with Abacus products. This foreclosure was grounded on the "best efforts" clause of Plaintiff's dealership contract. When Defendant learned of impending dealer expansion into competitive products, Abacus representatives would inform the dealer that an expansion would be a breach of the "best efforts" clause, and that hence its Abacus dealership would be in jeopardy. Defendant thus used the threatened loss of the entire Abacus line as leverage to foreclose Plaintiff from carrying competitive products. Thus, although on various occasions competitors of Abacus approached Brooks with a view towards Brooks marketing their products, until 1974 Brooks declined to do so because of the restrictions imposed by Abacus. Although Plaintiff had the opportunity, ability and incentive to expand its product lines, Plaintiff was foreclosed from doing so by the illegal restraints imposed on it by Defendant. Plaintiff thereby lost substantial sales and profits. In the absence of such a restriction, Plaintiff would have certainly carried a competing photocopier line, for which Plaintiff would have received additional net profits of at least $20,000 during the four years preceding the filing of the complaint.

B. Pretermination damages due to the territorial restrictions imposed on Plaintiff.

Abacus enforced both territorial and customer restrictions upon Plaintiff, and used its other dealers to police such restrictions. Defendant used the "best efforts" clause and the threat of termination for failure to comply with Defendant's interpretation of it as the principal means of coercing adherence to such restrictions. In addition, any sales made by Plaintiff outside its designated territory resulted in Plaintiff's having to pay over a punitive 50% of its commission to the dealer to whom the territory was assigned. Plaintiff had substantially expanded its business in 1971 when it opened its Hochdorf branch. That store provided it with a base for substantially expanding its sales into the Hemlock Falls area. Specifically, the southern portion of Hemlock Falls and the contiguous suburbs became the natural sales area for Plaintiff upon the opening of the Hochdorf store. From the opening of that store to the filing of the complaint, a reasonable estimate of Plaintiff's losses as a result of this restriction is $51,000. This estimate does not take into account additional lost sales and profits resulting from restrictions upon Plaintiff's sales in other areas outside its territory.

Plaintiff was also foreclosed by its contract with Abacus from making equipment sales to Franklin State University, which had previously been its largest single customer. A reasonable estimate of the losses resulting from that restriction in the four years preceding the filing of the complaint is $12,000.

C. Pretermination damages due to Defendant's conspiracy to fix retail prices.

Defendant conspired to fix resale prices of its equipment which it was firm and resolute in enforcing through a variety of mechanisms, e.g., continuous policing by Abacus field personnel and by other dealers, repeated exhortations by Abacus top brass at sales meetings, written instructions from Abacus to its dealers to sell only at suggested retail prices unless a departure therefrom was specifically authorized by Abacus, a warranty card system whereby the purchaser informed the warrantor (Abacus) of the price paid for the particular product, and threatened communication of termination of any dealer which did not adhere. Abacus maintained the prices of its products at unreasonably high levels, particularly during the recession of 1972-74, and potential customers were thereby lost by Brooks to those handling equipment manufactured by competitors of Abacus. The total amount of Plaintiff's losses of sales and profits over the years as a result of Abacus' illegal fixing of resale prices can never be known with certainty. However, a reasonable estimate of the lost profits incurred in 1973 and 1974 alone is $24,000.

D. Pretermination damages as a result of full line forcing.

Defendant was able to use its economic power to coerce Plaintiff into carrying Abacus products which it did not desire and which it was unable to sell effectively, by conditioning its sales of its desirable lines to purchasers by Plaintiff of undesirable products. Because of this illegal tie-in, Plaintiff suffered losses of substantial, unrecouped, out of pocket costs on sales of the Copier 1000 as well as incalculable lost good will from dissatisfied customers. The losses in out of pocket expenses alone amounted to $23,000.

E. Postermination damages.

Plaintiff's termination as an Abacus dealer was proximately caused by Plaintiff's failure to adhere to the illegal restrictions imposed on Plaintiff by Defendant. In addition, there was a conspiracy between Defendant and Farr, that if Plaintiff did not cease selling Abacus products from Plaintiff's Hochdorf store, Plaintiff's Abacus dealership would be terminated and Farr would take over Plaintiff's Abacus territory. Plaintiff is therefore entitled to recover damages suffered as a result of and proximately flowing from its illegal termination as an Abacus dealer. Such damages include losses of profits from the date of termination to the date of trial sustained from the territory assigned to Plaintiff, estimated as $105,000; lost profits from the sales that would have been made outside that territory during the same period, estimated at $43,000; and lost profits over that period in the future during which Plaintiff had a reasonable expectation of the dealership continuing, estimated at $326,000.

CONCLUSION:

As a result of Defendant's unlawful activities, Plaintiff has suffered injury to its business and property and has sustained substantial damages prior to and as a result of the unlawful termination of Defendant's dealership agreement with Plaintiff. Those damages total at least $602,000 before trebling.

December 1, 1976

Respectfully submitted,

STANDE & DELYVER
2130 Grand Avenue
Franklin City, Franklin
Attorneys for Plaintiff

IN THE UNITED STATES DISTRICT COURT FOR THE SOUTHERN DISTRICT OF FRANKLIN

. . . .

BROOKS OFFICE SUPPLY CO., INC.,	)))	
Plaintiff,	))	Civil Action No. 74 Civ. 1553
v.	))	
ABACUS, INC.,	)))	
Defendant.	)	

. . . .

DEFENDANT'S PRETRIAL NARRATIVE STATEMENT

AND NOW, comes Defendant, by their attorneys, Delahy, Lenger & Waite, and for its pretrial narrative statement states as follows:

I. Preliminary Legal Considerations

The pretrial narrative filed by Plaintiff only serves to highlight the serious legal defects in the many causes of action asserted by the Plaintiff. Defendant believes that, as a matter of law, based on the facts revealed in discovery, most if not all of Plaintiff's claims ought to be dismissed. Defendant will not in this narrative address itself to these legal arguments but will instead seek to advance them through appropriate motions.

Finally, Defendant does not now propose to rebut the damage computations contained in Plaintiff's pretrial narrative. It is defendant's position that plaintiff has suffered no injury and that the calculations offered in Plaintiff's expert's report which accompanied the pretrial narrative are inconsistent, improperly prepared or legally inadmissible for other reasons. Additionally, there remain open several requests for additional discovery on matters relating to the issues of damages. Without answers to these discovery matters a full analysis of the damage issue is impossible.

II. Defendant's Factual Position

Simply stated, the facts are that defendant terminated the dealership arrangement with Brooks Office Supply Co. ("Brooks") for valid business reasons in a proper and lawful manner. Defendant's marketing policies both nationally and as applied to Brooks have always complied with the antitrust laws of the United States. Plaintiff simply has no cause of action for damages against the defendant.

A. The Corporate Structure of Abacus, Inc.

Abacus, Inc. is a Delaware corporation with headquarters in San Francisco, California. Since 1962 it has been a wholly owned subsidiary of Abacus International, an international corporation engaged in a variety of industrial and commercial activities on a world-wide scale. Abacus, Inc. ("Abacus") is principally engaged in the importation and marketing in the United States of industrial and commercial equipment.

Abacus is subdivided into several functional divisions at the national level, and these divisions are further subdivided into regions and districts. The Office Machine Division is the one whose activities are the subject of this lawsuit. This division formulates and implements general marketing policy on a national level with regard to office equipment lines including electronic calculators, cash registers, typewriters, dictating and transcribing systems and desk photocopiers. Mr. Harold R. George is the General Manager of the Office Machine Divsion. The National Director of Marketing is Mr. Bernard D. White. Mr. White is primarily responsible for implementation of sales policy. The Abacus office machine marketing operation is divided into regions with Regional Directors who report to Mr. White. The Midwest Region consists of the states of Franklin, Iowa, Kansas, Minnesota, North Dakota, South Dakota, Nebraska and Missouri. Mr. William H. Soule is the Midwest Regional Director. Mr. Soule's principal function is to coordinate the marketing activities at the regional level. He has primary responsibility for the Abacus dealership program in the region and supervises district dealer representatives. Districts are primarily determined by market considerations. The entire State of Franklin is a single district. The dealer representative for the Franklin District is Mr. Richard N. Hines. Mr. Hines' duties consist of liaison with the dealers in the District. The Plaintiff, Brooks Office Supply Co., a corporation owned principally by Mr. Rufus B. Brooks II, was, prior to September 30, 1974, a franchised Abacus dealer in the Franklin District.

B. The Termination of Brooks

Brooks sold various types of office machines and equipment which were imported and distributed by the defendant. The agreement governing the sale of this equipment was a customary dealership agreement which was in effect for successive one-year terms. The agreement contained, in addition, a cancellation provision similar to the provisions common throughout industry.

Generally, in the period of time from 1968 to 1971 or 1972, Brooks did an adequate job of selling Abacus' equipment. It generally met its quota and in some years it exceeded its quota. Customer complaints did occur and Brooks obviously had employee turnover problems. Nonetheless, as long as sales coverage and service was reasonably adequate no reason existed for Abacus to consider a new marketing arrangement to replace its arrangement with Brooks.

Beginning in approximately 1972 the performance of Brooks in representing Abacus began to deteriorate. Not only did sales fall but customer complaints increased. Abacus' personnel reviewed these matters on many occasions with the president of Brooks. While even today it is difficult to know the precise reason for the clear inadequacy of Brooks' performance, a number of factors appear to have contributed to deterioration in sales. Brooks' problems in holding capable employees increased. The quality of its service was reported to have been much less than adequate. Customer complaints increasingly occurred. It may be that the technology of a new generation of electronic equipment was beyond the technical capabilities of the top management of Brooks, notwithstanding the service training provided by Abacus. At the same time that the performance for Abacus was deteriorating, the sales of other products by Brooks was increasing. Moreover, Brooks' president was obviously devoting time and effort of the organization to the development of new financial ventures, and was often absent when the Abacus district representative called at Brooks.

Abacus personnel repeatedly expressed concern to the president of Brooks. Customer complaints, the precipitous decline in sales by Brooks and the continuing preoccupation of Brooks' management in efforts other than the sales of Brooks' products were all discussed. Notwithstanding this Brooks' performance continued to deteriorate. While the general economy was soft in 1973 and 1974, other Abacus dealers performed as well or better than expected. This was not true of Brooks. Its performance stood out as a significant failure. Intensive counselling and efforts to work with Brooks in 1973 met with no success. Finally, when new orders had not even reached $65,000 as of the end of June 1974, it became necessary for Abacus' management to terminate the relationship with Brooks and make alternate plans for the marketing of their products.

No representations or misrepresentations were made concerning the continued renewal of the Brooks agreement. No anticompetitive reasons influenced the decision to terminate the relationship. The expert report attached hereto demonstrates dramatically that the instinctive business observations of the Abacus' management at the time the termination decision was made are backed by ample empirical data.

C. Alleged Restraints on Trade

Price Fixing

Plaintiff's claim involving price fixing is based primarily on an effort to confuse Abacus' policy on reducing the price charged *to* the dealer with its policy on the retail prices charged *by* dealers. Dealers purchased equipment from Abacus at a cost calculated by taking a discount from the suggested list price for Abacus' equipment. This method for computing the dealer's cost is common throughout American industry. The crucial fact is, however, that dealers were free to resell products at any price which they desired to set. In fact, depositions of other Abacus dealers revealed that they did sell products at a price other than the "list price". Abacus did not encourage its dealers, especially its smaller dealers, to regularly sell at less than the suggested list price, because of its concern that such dealers would then have insufficient financial ability and incentive to provide an adequate level of customer service. But every dealer was free to sell at any price he chose.

While the dealer normally purchased at a dealer cost computed by taking the discount from the published list price, Abacus did institute a policy under which the dealer might obtain a reduction in his cost where he was confronted with competition from products made by other manufacturers. Under this procedure Brooks and other dealers would from time to time obtain a lower dealer cost from Abacus to better enable them to meet competition. In an effort to concoct a cause of action based on "price fixing", plaintiff seeks to misconstrue this policy designed to assist dealers, especially its smaller dealers such as Brooks, to meet competition.

Full Line Forcing

Abacus markets and sells several different lines of equipment. For marketing purposes these products were grouped together in categories reflecting the type of equipment and its market uses. Thus, office equipment which would be primarily used in commercial applications was placed under the responsibility of one division. Equipment which would normally be used for scientific and analytical applications was placed under the responsibility of another marketing division. The equipment in each of these various product groups would generally be sold to the same type of customer for similar and related applications. Naturally the same customer, especially in the case of large corporations and some governmental entities, might well have installations which needed equipment from more than one of the Abacus product groups. In some such cases, Abacus designated the customer as a national account and dealt with it directly rather than through local dealers.

In its marketing effort, each division sought the best possible representation for the products in its group. In some cases this meant marketing through manufacturer's representatives; in other cases it meant marketing through dealers. When the marketing outlet was chosen, it would assume responsibility for marketing all of the products in the product group. In the case of dealers, Abacus undertook to identify the dealer as the Abacus representative for that product group in all its promotional and advertising efforts which would likely reach customers in the dealer's area. Nevertheless, no dealer was ever forced to take on a product line.

In the specific case of the Copier 1000/2000 product line, Brooks actively sought to become the Abacus representative for that product line. Brooks willingly and knowingly undertook to purchase demonstration equipment in an effort to market this new line.

Restrictions on Sales of Other Products

The record is crystal clear that other Abacus dealers throughout the country regularly represented and still do represent many manufacturers other than Abacus. Indeed, numerous Abacus dealers also sell and have sold equipment which was competitive with products made and sold by Abacus. Abacus' sole interest was in achieving what it believed to be adequate sales through its various marketing outlets.

Territorial Restrictions

The equipment and apparatus which is involved in this lawsuit is sophisticated, sensitive and expensive. In fact in most cases dealers do not even take possession of the equipment which is shipped directly from Abacus to the user.

From Abacus' standpoint they have devoted millions of dollars to research and development and they market one of the finest lines of office equipment available in the United States. In addition to their enormous research and development effort they have expended large sums of money on patent and trademark protection for their product line. In addition to normal advertising expenses they sponsor technical training schools for dealers and their employees. Through these efforts Abacus has achieved an excellent name and valuable goodwill in this industry.

Much of Abacus' equipment must be installed by the manufacturer or its marketing representative in a manner to assure that it is properly functioning at the customer's facility. On the larger computerized cash register systems proper installation may take two to three working days for a serviceman. In addition to the fact that such equipment must be properly installed if it is to function for its designed purpose, continuing service is of vital importance to the customer. Prompt service is vital to the maintenance of Abacus' name and goodwill.

From the customer's standpoint when purchasing new equipment they are concerned with both the capability of the equipment and with being assured that the seller will properly install and adjust the equipment and promptly provide needed service so that the equipment achieves the result desired by the customer. Naturally if equipment does not have the capability to meet the purpose set by the customer, it will not be considered. Equally important, however, is the fact that if the customer is not satisfied that the equipment will be properly installed, adjusted and serviced he will not purchase the equipment.

In its marketing program Abacus has been acutely aware of the fact that the demonstrated excellence of its products is not enough. Customers must be assured that equipment which they purchase will be properly installed and that needed maintenance and repairs will be promptly performed. This factor is so obvious that Abacus dealers, competitors and customers all recognize the interrelationship of sales and service.

Because of this relationship, under the Abacus marketing program all of its dealers assume responsibility for both sales and service. Of necessity this means that each dealer must limit the area in which it operates to an area where its customers' needs can be properly served. Indeed, from the dealer's standpoint, it makes no sense to regularly market beyond an area where installation and service can be economically provided.

The treatment of the territorial clause in the Abacus agreement (and the location clause which serves partially to implement it) demonstrates that they have pursued a reasonable policy. Territory lines have not been rigidly enforced. Occasionally sales are made outside of a dealer's territory and no dealer has ever been terminated for selling outside of its territory. Indeed, a formal policy was established to permit a sharing of profits in a situation where one dealer makes a sale in one area of the country for the installation and service of that equipment in a different area of the country.

While the Abacus policy of having its marketing outlets concentrate on those areas where they can provide effective service in addition to sales coverage is not an unreasonable restriction on trade; it has had the effect in the case of Brooks of affording profits to that organization which it would not have been likely to have achieved through its own efforts. The outstanding name and the superiority of Abacus products have led many customers to purchase equipment within the area served by Brooks without any sales effort on the part of Brooks.

The Conspiracy Allegations

Plaintiff seeks to fabricate a conspiracy between Defendant and Farr, the dealer appointed to replace Plaintiff. However, the record already made in the course of discovery makes crystal clear that Abacus management unilaterally decided, for adequate business reasons, that Brooks' progressively deteriorating performance made it no longer acceptable as the Abacus dealer in that area. Similarly, Abacus management unilaterally decided that Farr's continuing record of successful performance in an adjacent area in both sales and service, together with Farr's successful marketing of the Copier and dictation lines in the area-in which Brooks was located, indicated that Farr would represent Abacus effectively as to other lines in that area. There was no reason for a conspiracy. There are no facts even suggesting the existence of a conspiracy. There was no conspiracy.

III. Conclusion

Should any of the issues raised by Plaintiff's complaint ultimately be submitted to a jury for consideration, Defendant believes that the evidence will demonstrate that no violation of the antitrust laws occurred.

January 3, 1977   Respectfully submitted,

DELAHY, LENGER & WAITE
3715 Enterprise Tower
Franklin City, Franklin
    Attorneys for Defendant

APPENDIX V

ABACUS, INC.
750 S. Fulton Street
San Francisco, California

Compliance with the Anti-trust Laws

Purpose:

This section provides information and guidelines to employees of the Company concerning the Company's policy with respect to the anti-trust laws of the United States and, where applicable, the anti-trust laws of foreign governments.

Background

The anti-trust laws seek to preserve a free competitive economy in trade among the several United States and in commerce of the States with foreign countries. It is the Company's conviction that preservation of a competitive economy is essential to the public interest, the interest of the business community at large and of the Company individually.

Furthermore, anti-trust litigation can be very costly in time, money and effort. Violations of the anti-trust laws can, among other things, subject the Company involved to the imposition of injunctions, treble damages, and heavy fines. Individual employees can receive heavy fines or even be imprisoned.

Policy

It is the express policy of the Company to comply strictly in all respects with the anti-trust laws. This policy is not to be compromised or qualified by anyone acting for or on behalf of the Company.

It is the individual obligation of all Company personnel to comply with the policy and guidelines contained in this statement. Variation from this memorandum, where dictated by prudence and legitimate business considerations in particular situations, must be cleared by the Company's Chief Executive Officer with advice of counsel. Violation of this policy and guidelines may subject the individual to disciplinary action and, in the case of intentional or grossly negligent conduct, to dismissal.

Source: *Antitrust Law Journal* (American Bar Assoc.), Vol. 46, Issue 1 (1977)

Pricing

Company prices must be determined independently, in light of Company costs, market conditions and competitive prices. While competitive prices are legitimate bases for consideration in determining our own prices, they should be obtained only from non-competitive sources, such as published lists and data available to customers. Therefore, it is contrary to Company policy to send or receive any price list to or from a competitor, or to exchange with, or communicate to, a competitor any information concerning past, present or future bids, prices, discounts or terms and conditions of sale.

Sales to Competitors

In those circumstances where a competitor is a customer or a supplier of the Company, it is permissible to discuss or agree upon prices charged to or by the Company solely in transactions with that competitor. However, it is still against Company policy to discuss or agree in any way upon prices or any other terms or conditions in transaction by the Company or the competitor or anyone else with third parties.

Trade Associations

There is significant anti-trust risk in membership in a trade association because they involve meetings of, and joint action by, competitors. In addition, meetings of trade associations lend themselves to informal discussions of business matters which can be dangerous to Company personnel and to the Company. Therefore, it shall be the policy of the Company that there be no membership in a trade association, whether of manufacturers or of customers, without the advance specific written approval of the Group Vice President.

Relations with Customers and Suppliers

As a general rule, the Company is free to select its own customers and suppliers, including its franchised dealers. But it must do so independently. Any understanding or agreement—whether formal or informal, express or implied—to do or refrain from doing business with a third party is against Company policy. While, of course, usual credit sources may still be consulted in reaching independent decisions to deal with another company, such sources do not include the credit or any other department of a competitor.

Refusal to Deal

The Company is generally free to refuse to do business when it so desires. However, the General Counsel should be consulted before the Company refuses to sell to any customer or prospective customer (whether or not the Company has done business with the party in the past) other than for valid credit reasons approved by the Vice President-General Manager, since refusals to sell frequently lead to litigations. A written record should be maintained setting forth the basis for any decision not to sell to a customer or a prospective customer. The General Counsel should be consulted in any situation where litigation is threatened.

Agreements

To minimize anti-trust risk, the General Counsel should also be consulted before the Company enters into any new distribution or supply agreement (other than a simple, short-term buy-sell agreement) which differs in any respect from one previously approved.

Resale Price Maintenance

The Company is permitted to *suggest* to customers resale prices and terms or other marketing practices. However, unless a product is fair-traded, it is against Company policy to have any agreement—formal or informal, express or implied—concerning the prices or terms of resale of the customer. Furthermore, it makes no difference whether the agreement is aimed at higher or lower prices. It is up to the customer using his independent business judgment, to decide whether to follow the Company's suggestions. There must be no requirement that the customer adhere to the Company's suggestions and it is against Company policy for continued dealings with the customer to depend on such adherence to our suggestions.

Reciprocity

It is against Company policy to engage in reciprocity, that is, basing our purchases from a supplier upon the supplier's patronage of us. This includes all express or implied conditions or agreements. Of course, the Company may sell its products to one of our suppliers, but the sales and purchasing responsibilities of Company personnel should not be related to one another; each should separately assure that the Company's profits will be maximized.

Robinson-Patman Act

The provisions of the Robinson-Patman Act are particularly complex; they relate to direct and indirect price discrimination between customers. To enable counsel to review the Company's pricing structure and to alert personnel to possible Robinson-Patman problems, all new price lists and new promotional plans should be reviewed in advance. Any deviation from current price lists or from promotional plans should also be reviewed in advance by the General Counsel.